LED light tubes, computer,
DMX controller, electronics,
speakers
Dimensions variable

2005 - 2010

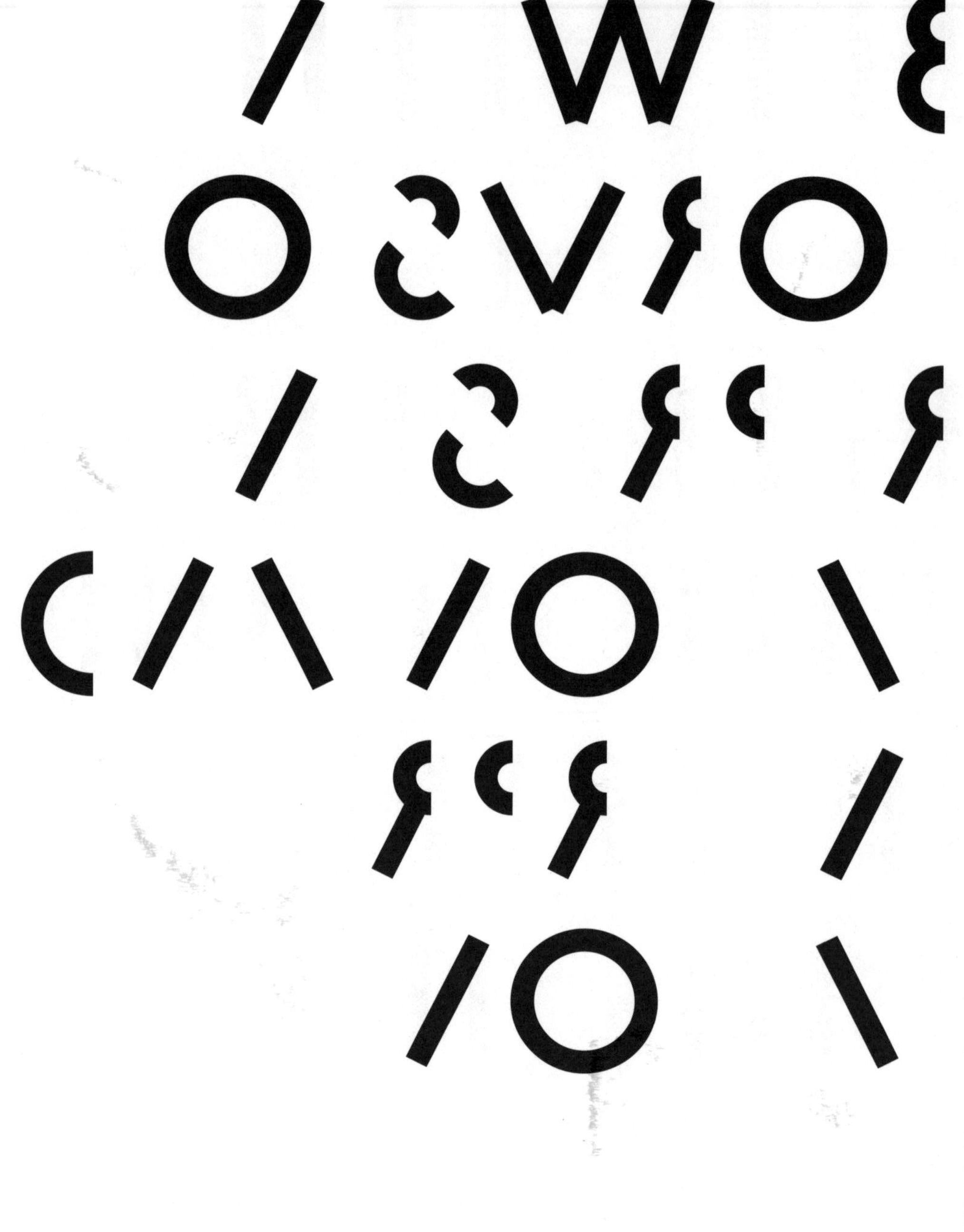

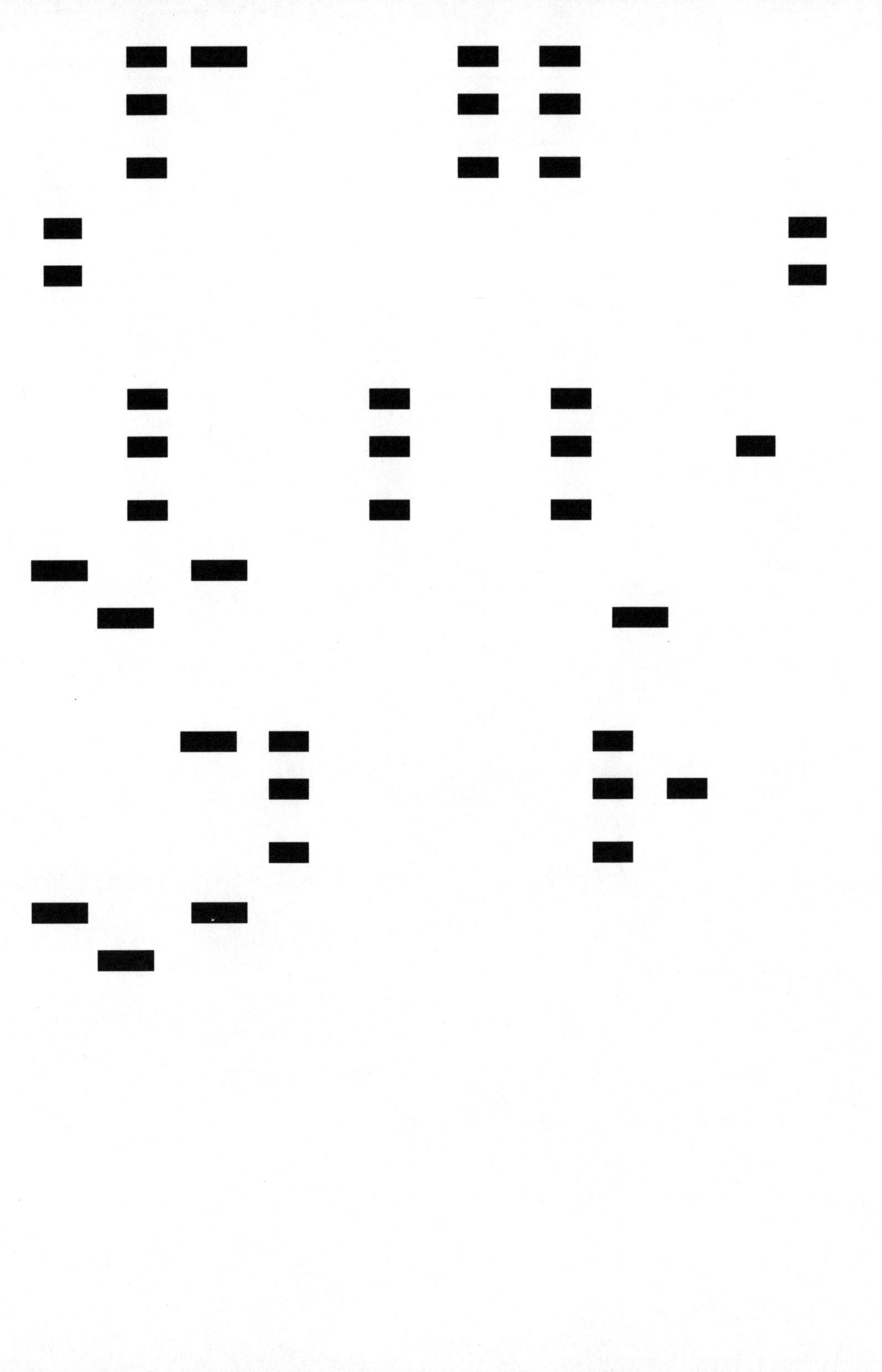

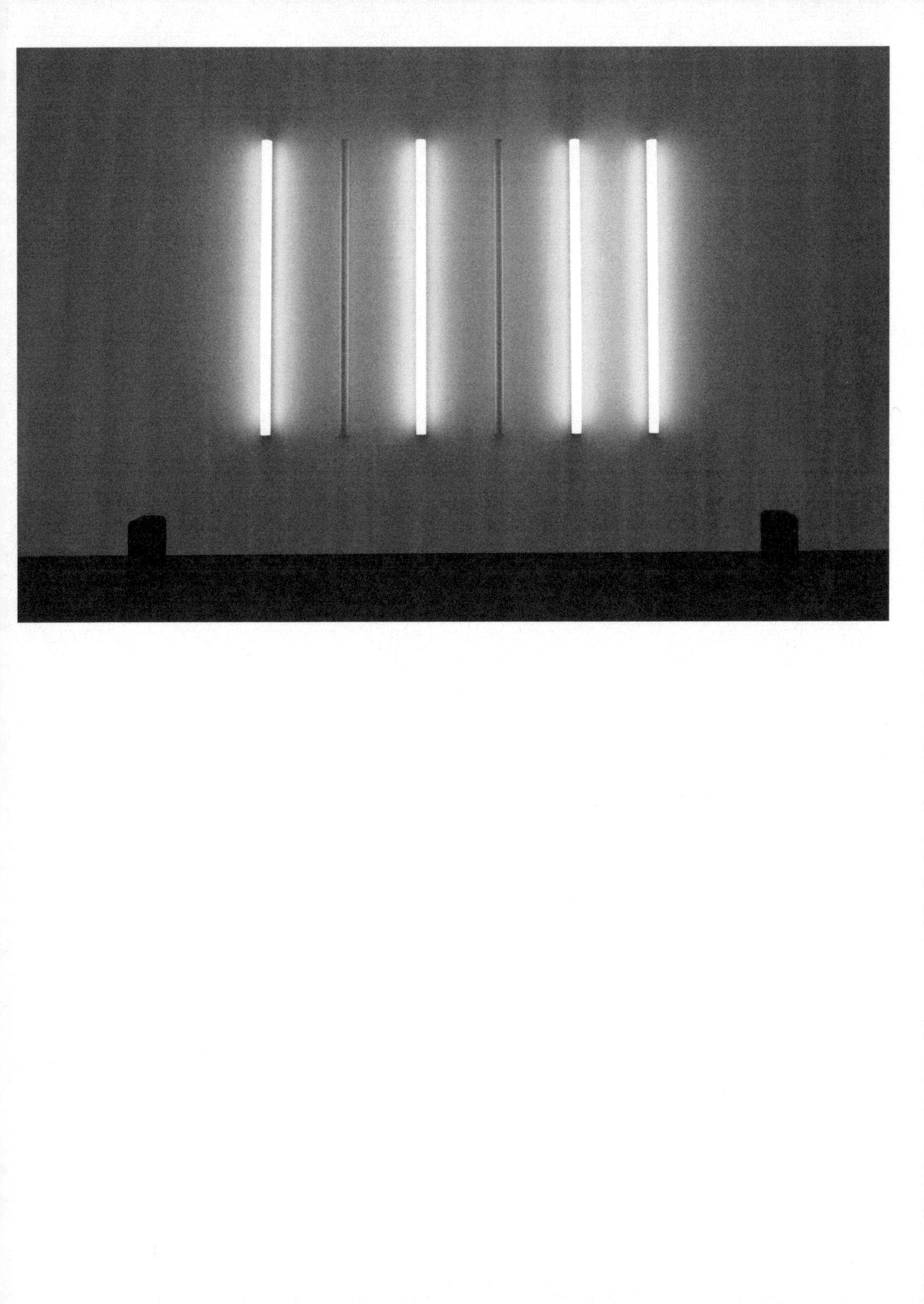

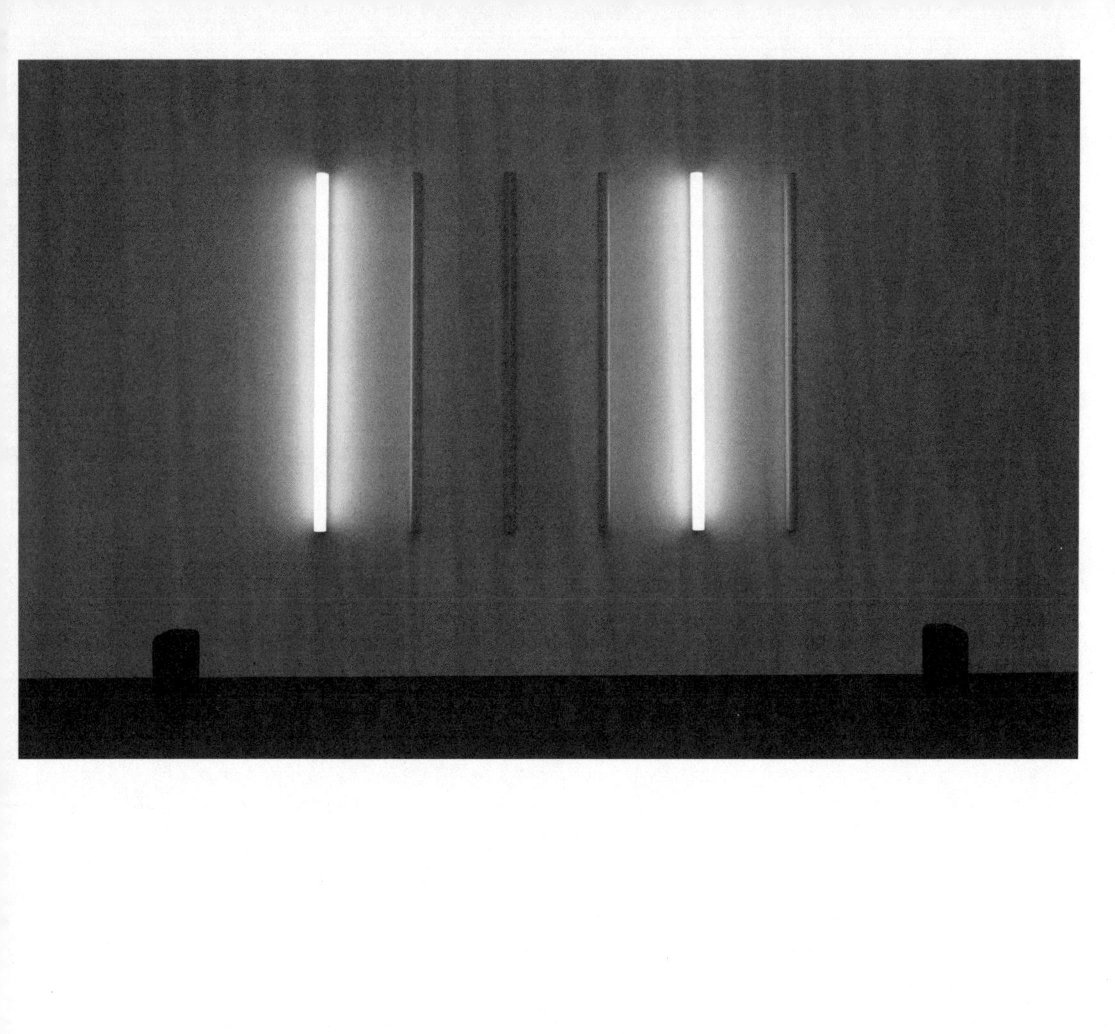

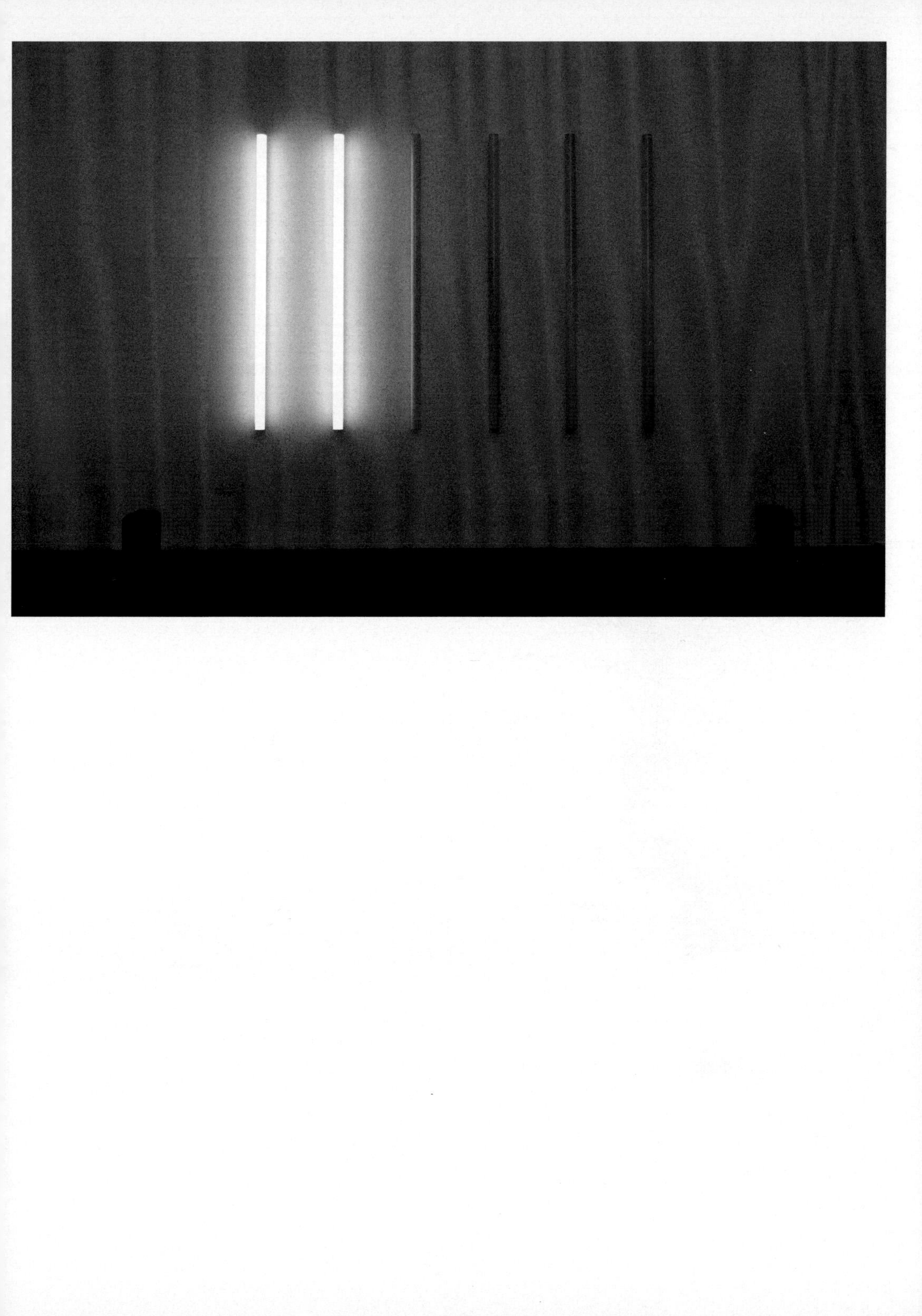

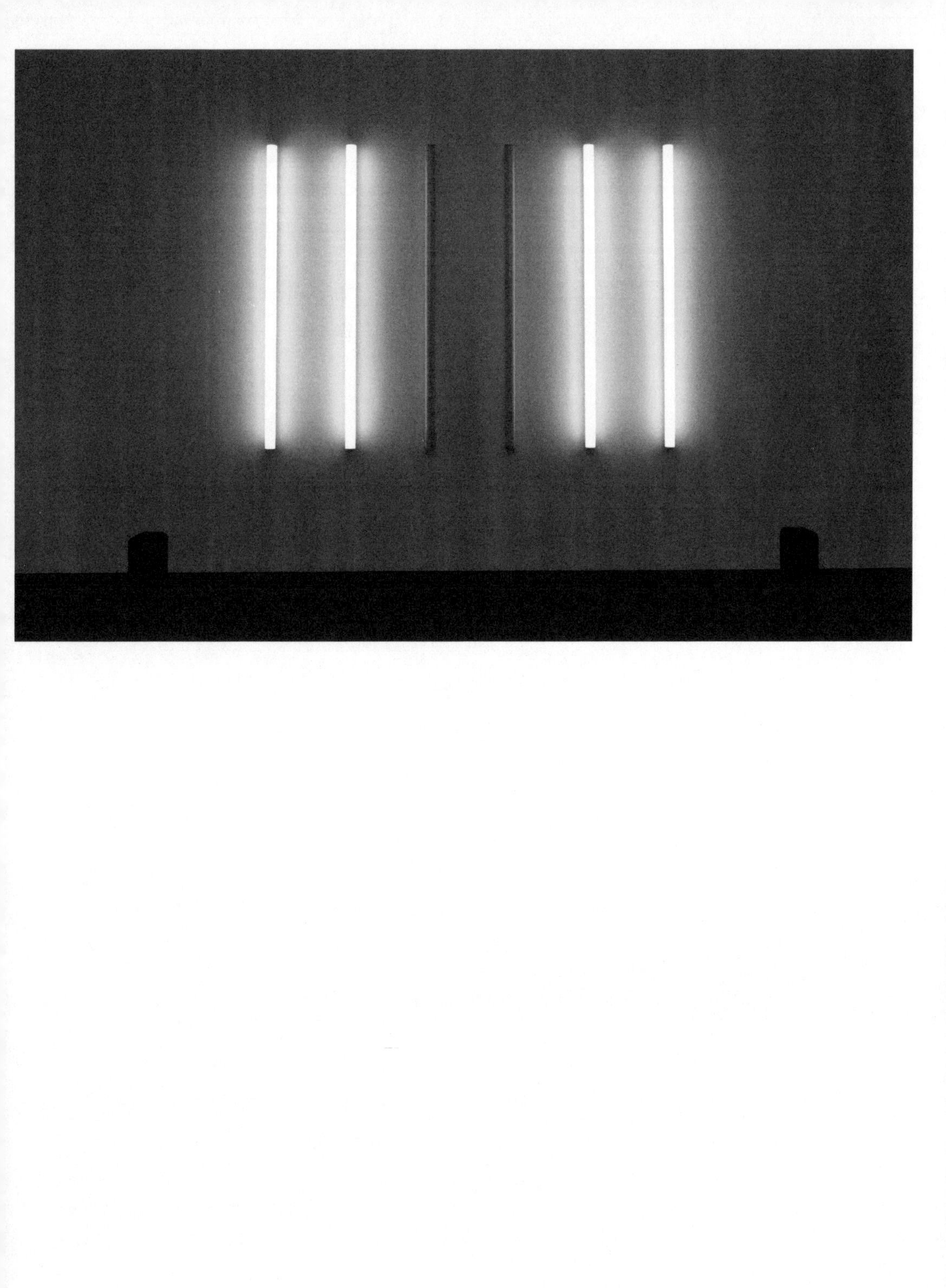

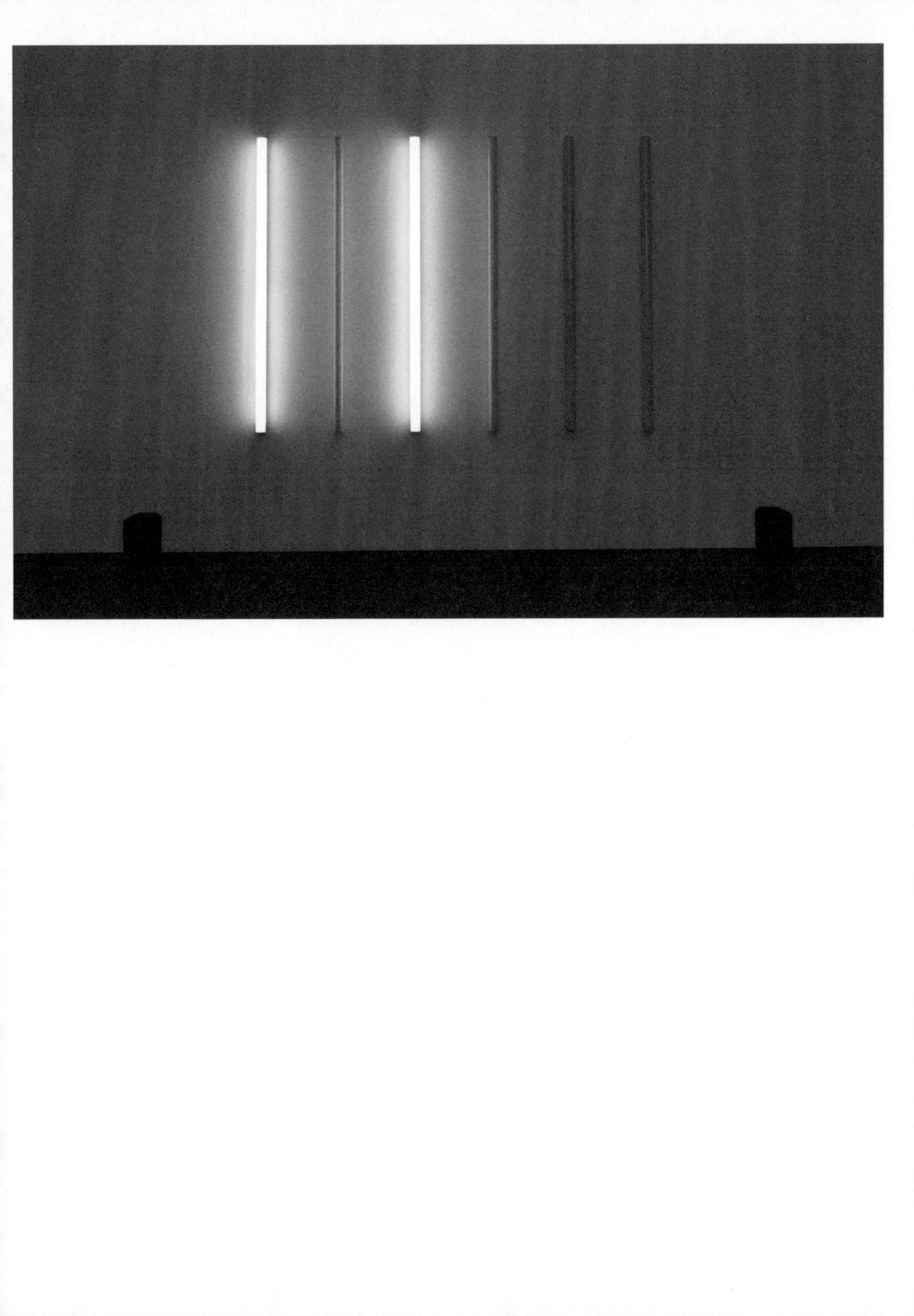

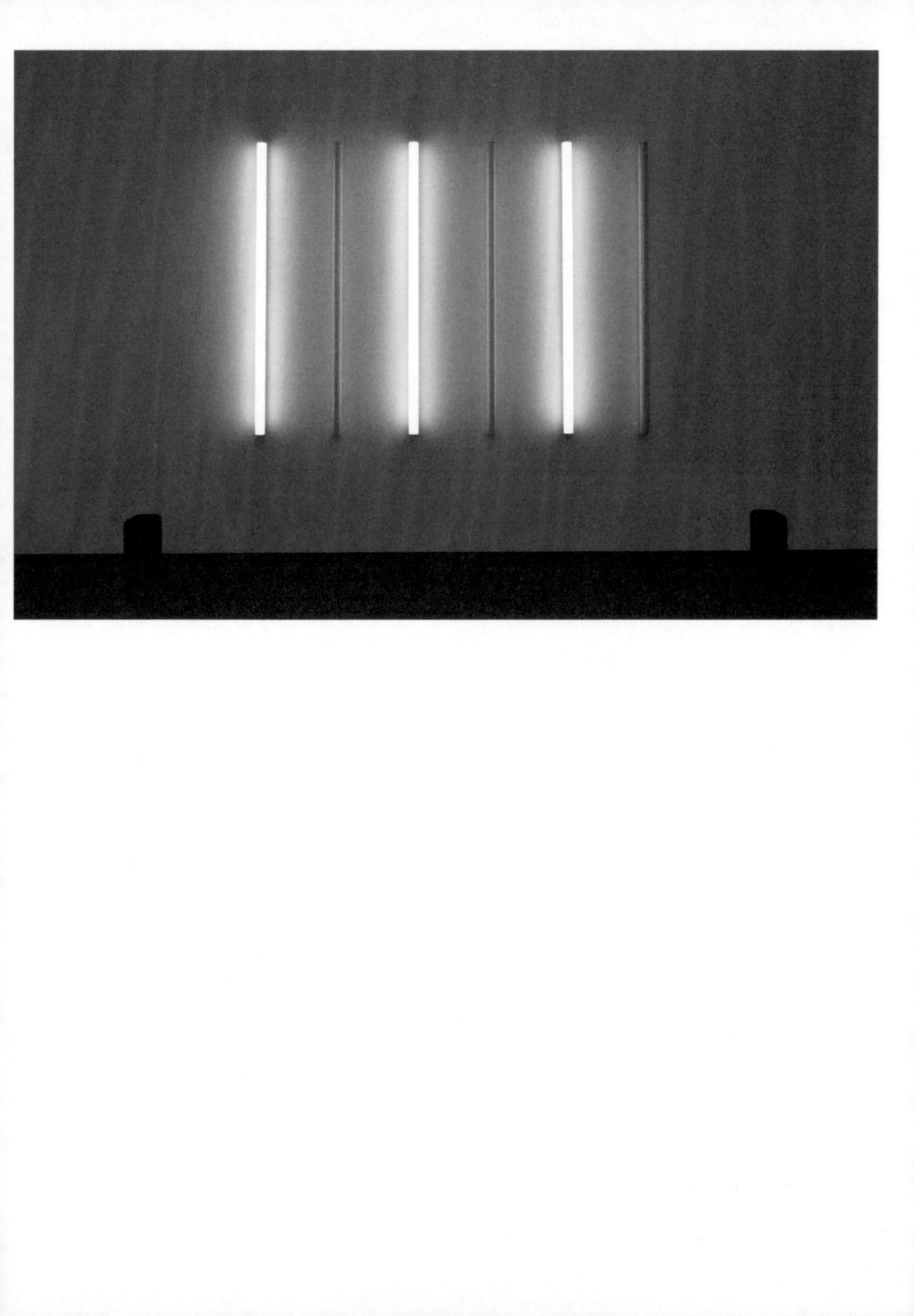

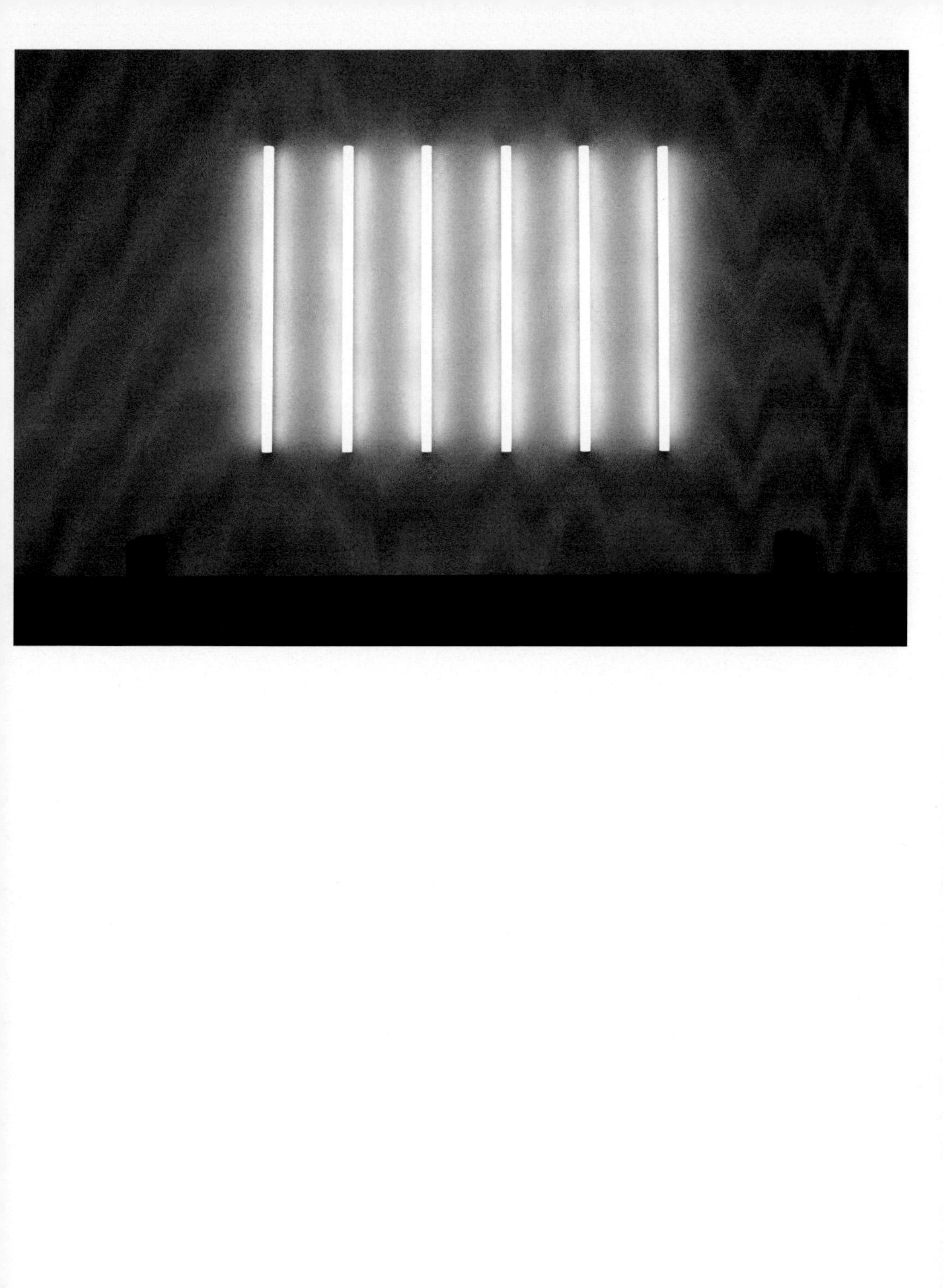

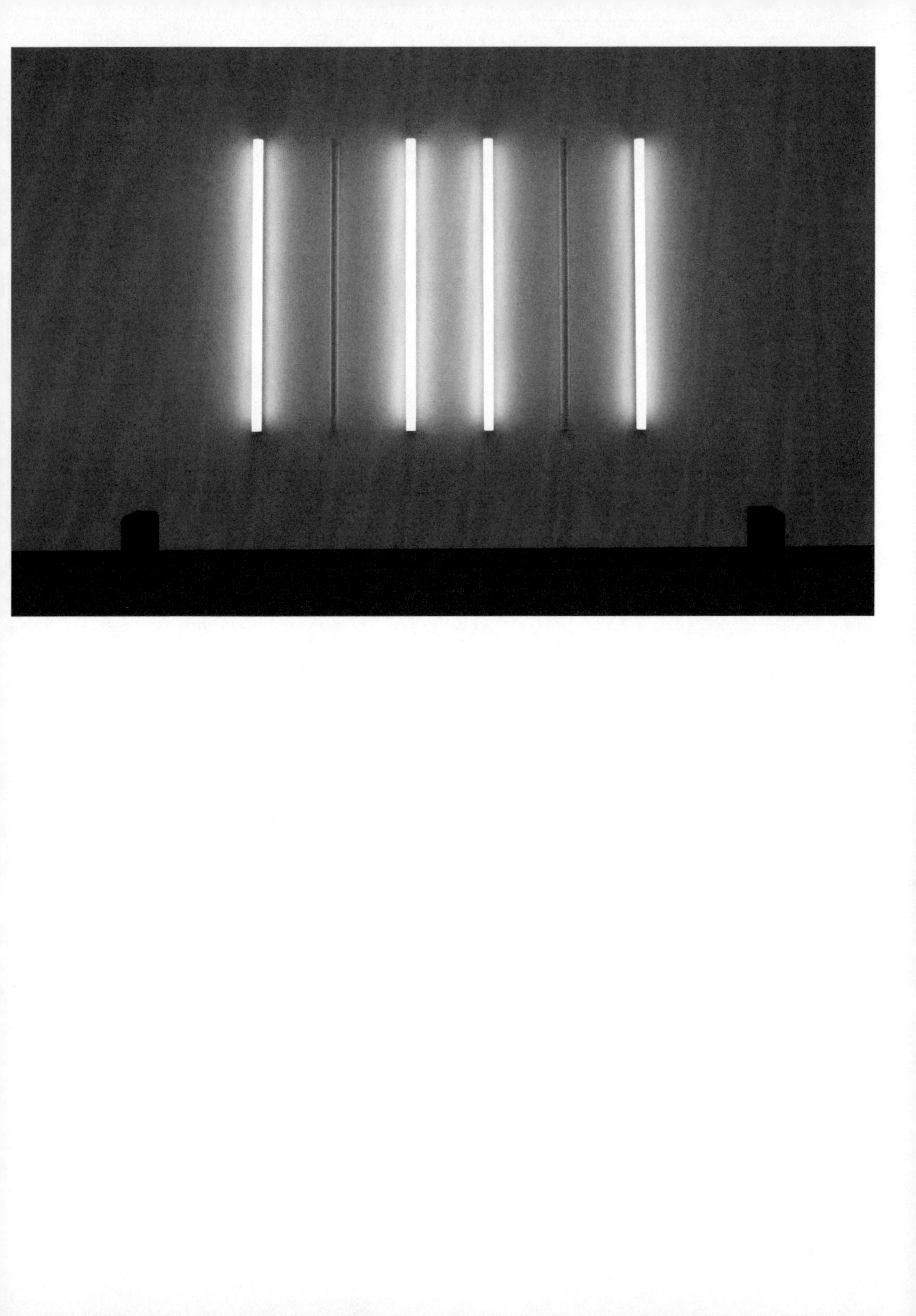

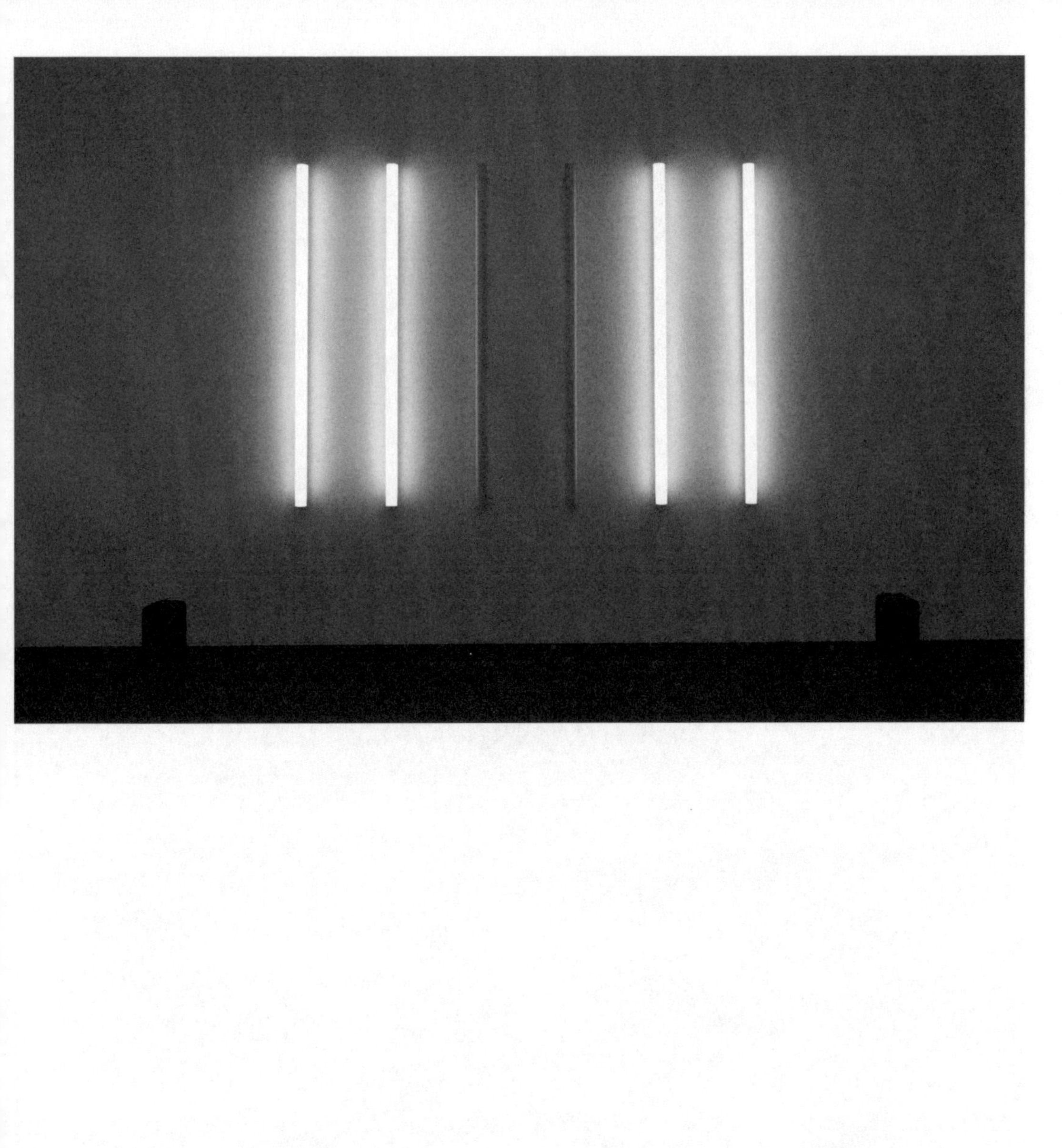

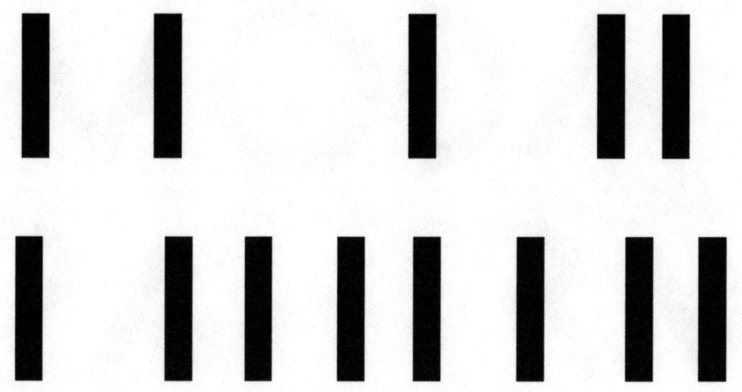

Double video projection
& single channel video,
black/white, sound,
23 mins
Dimensions variable

2006

ICOV

VOI

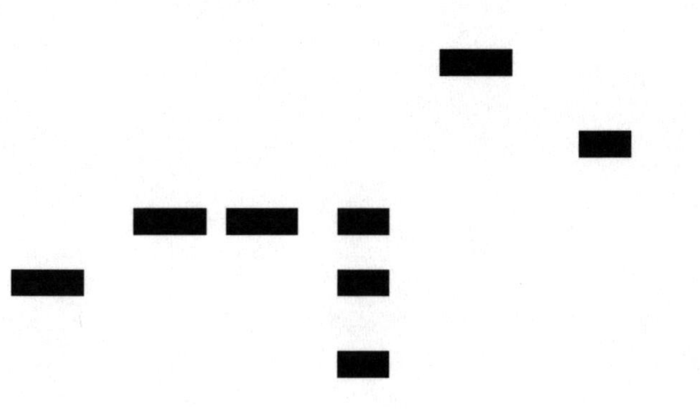

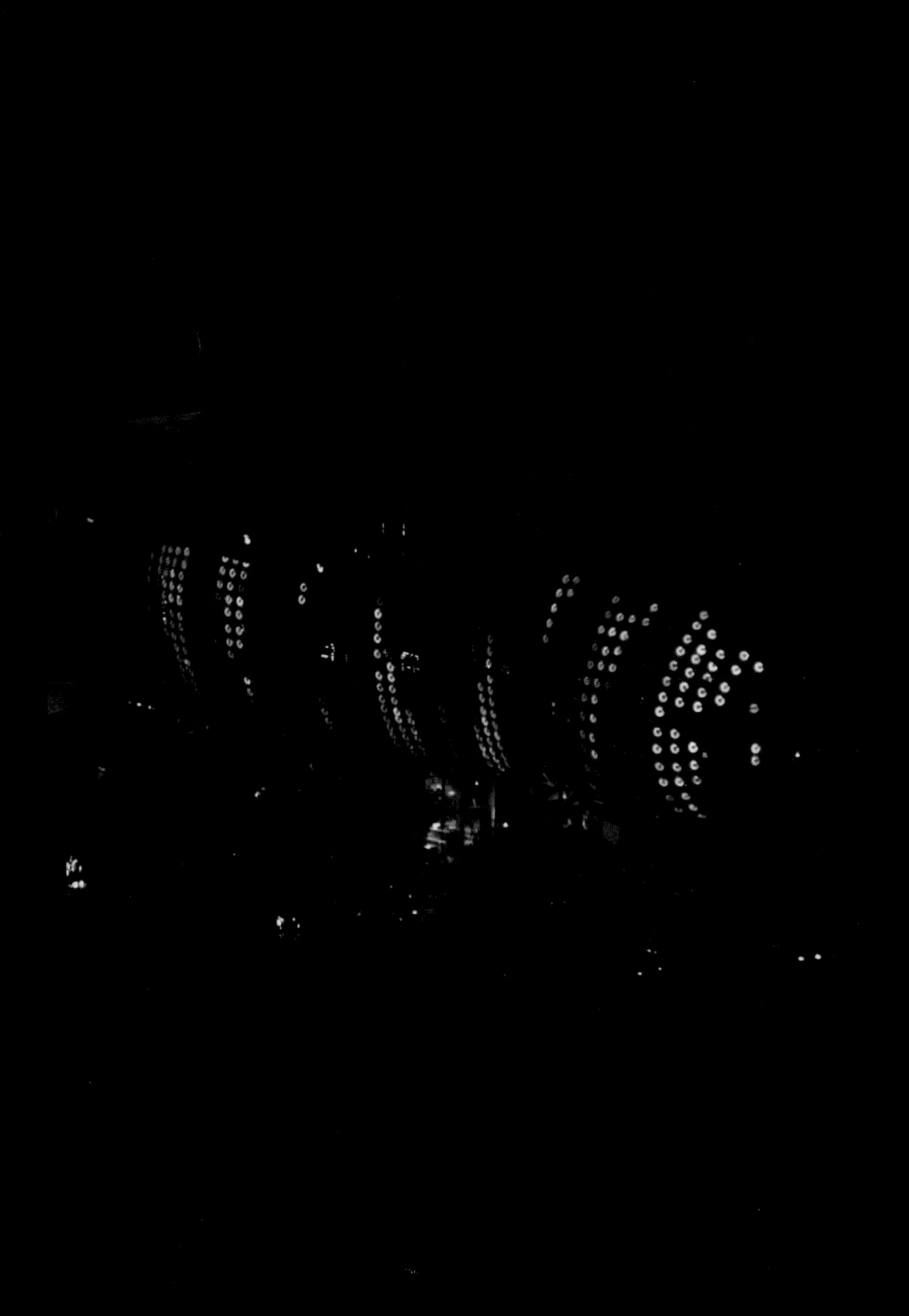

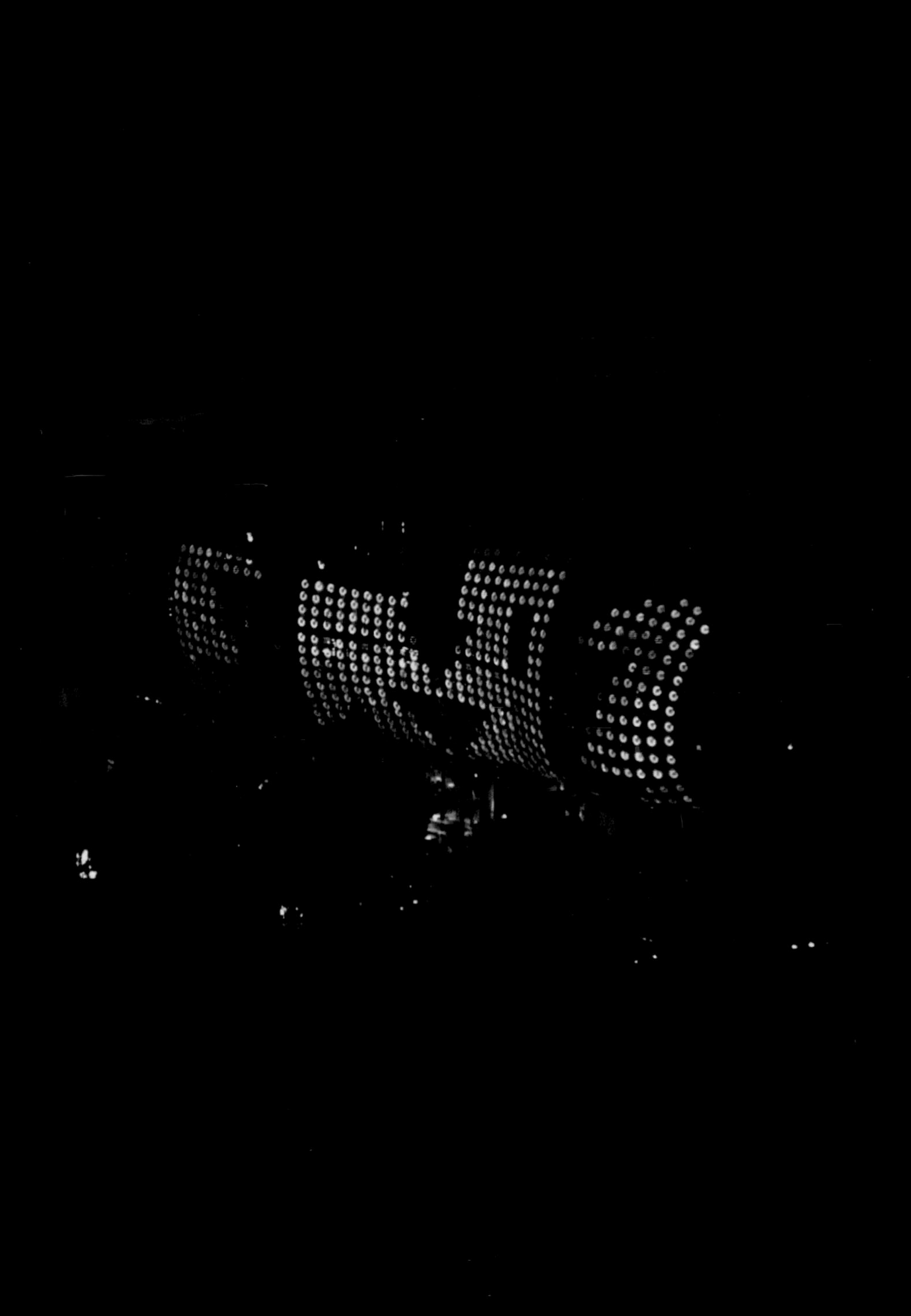

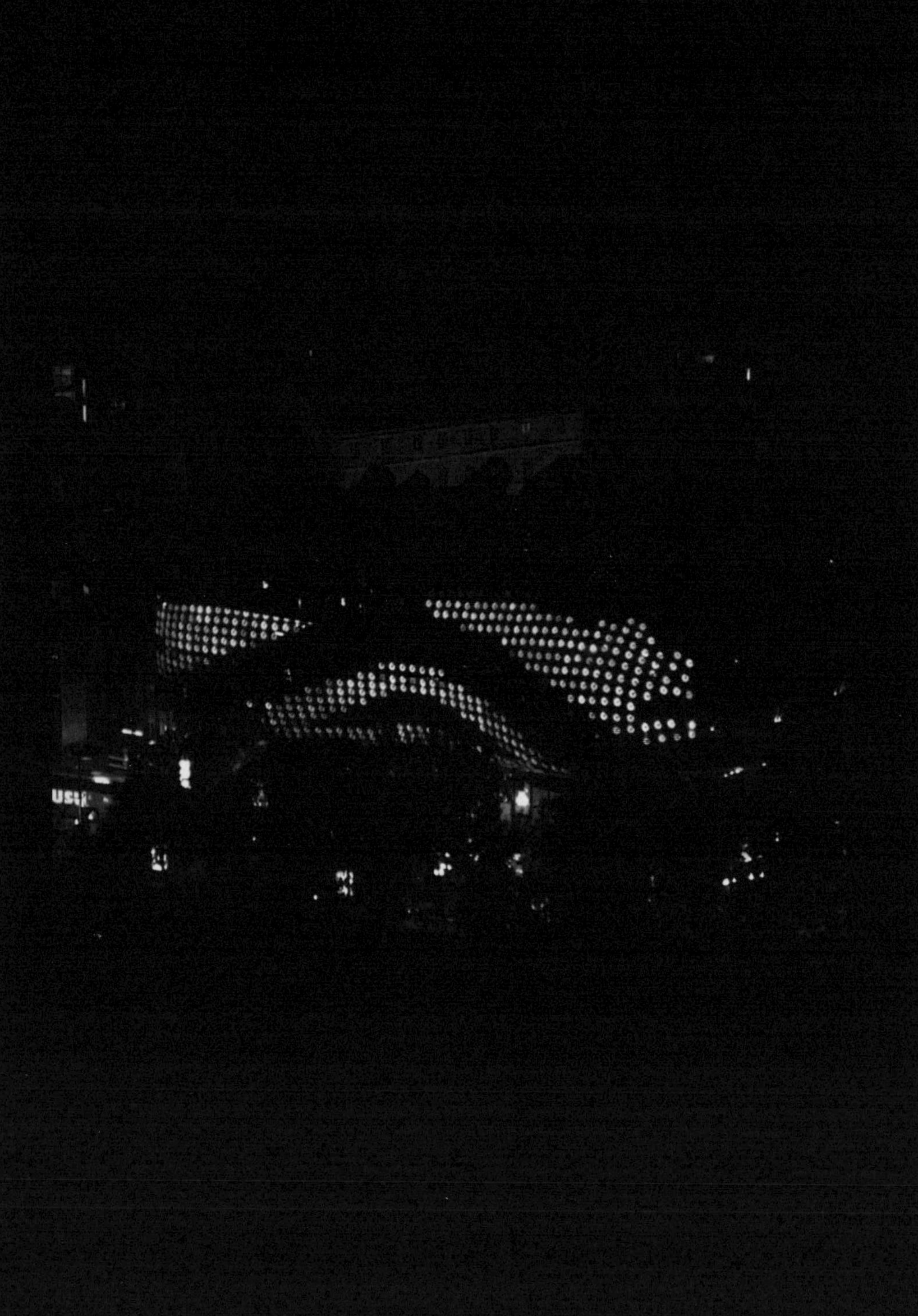

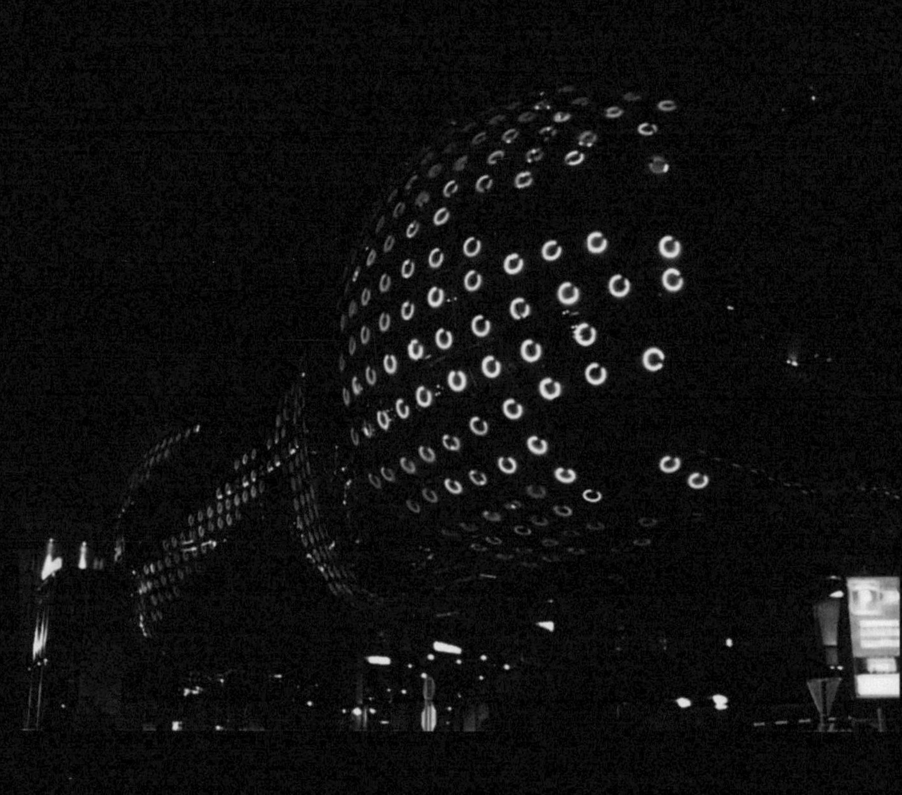

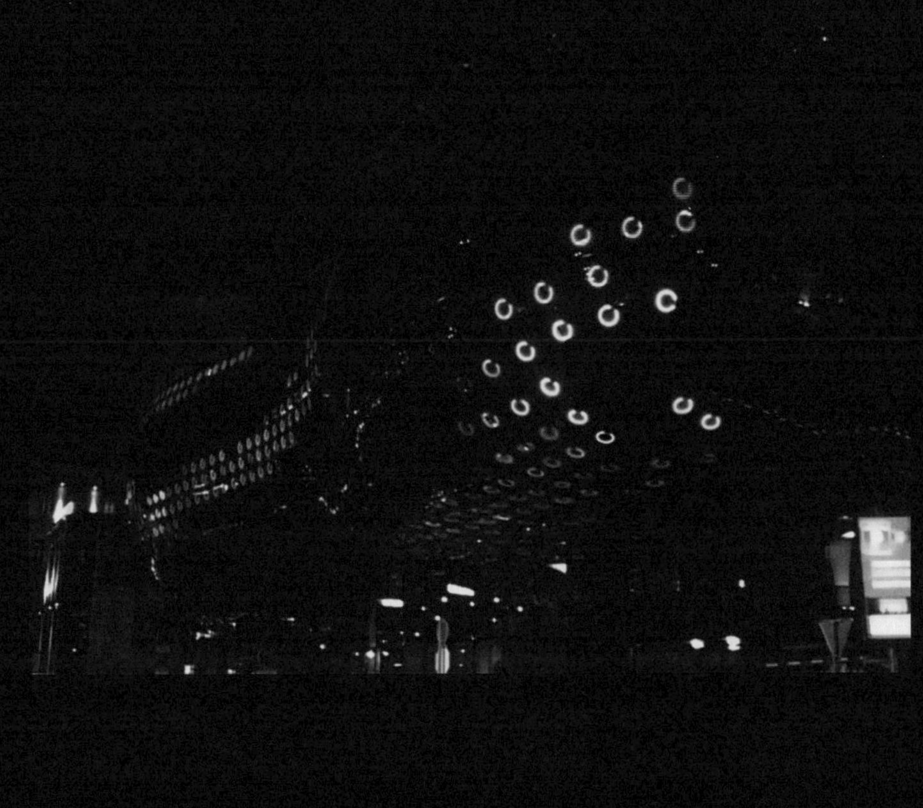

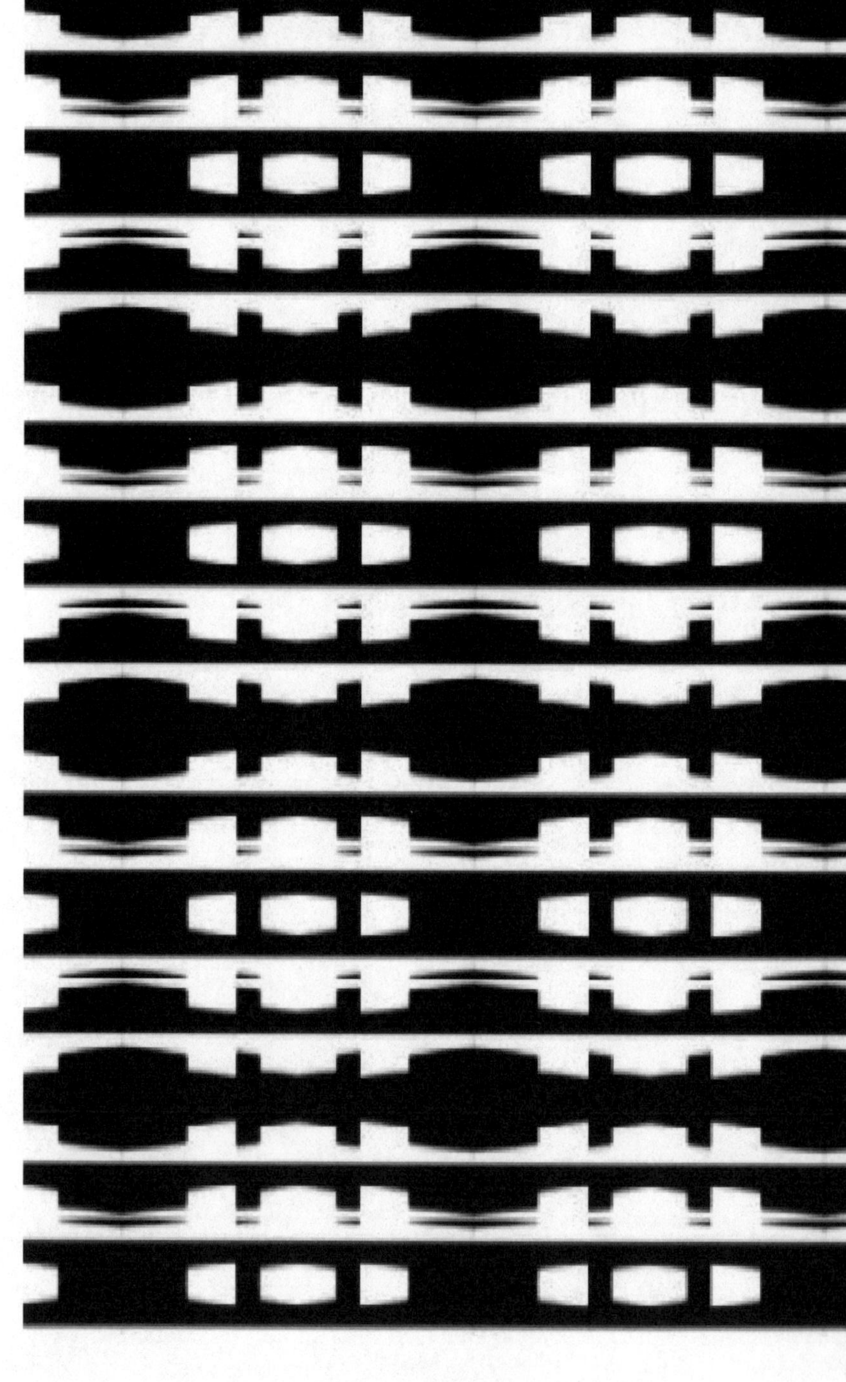

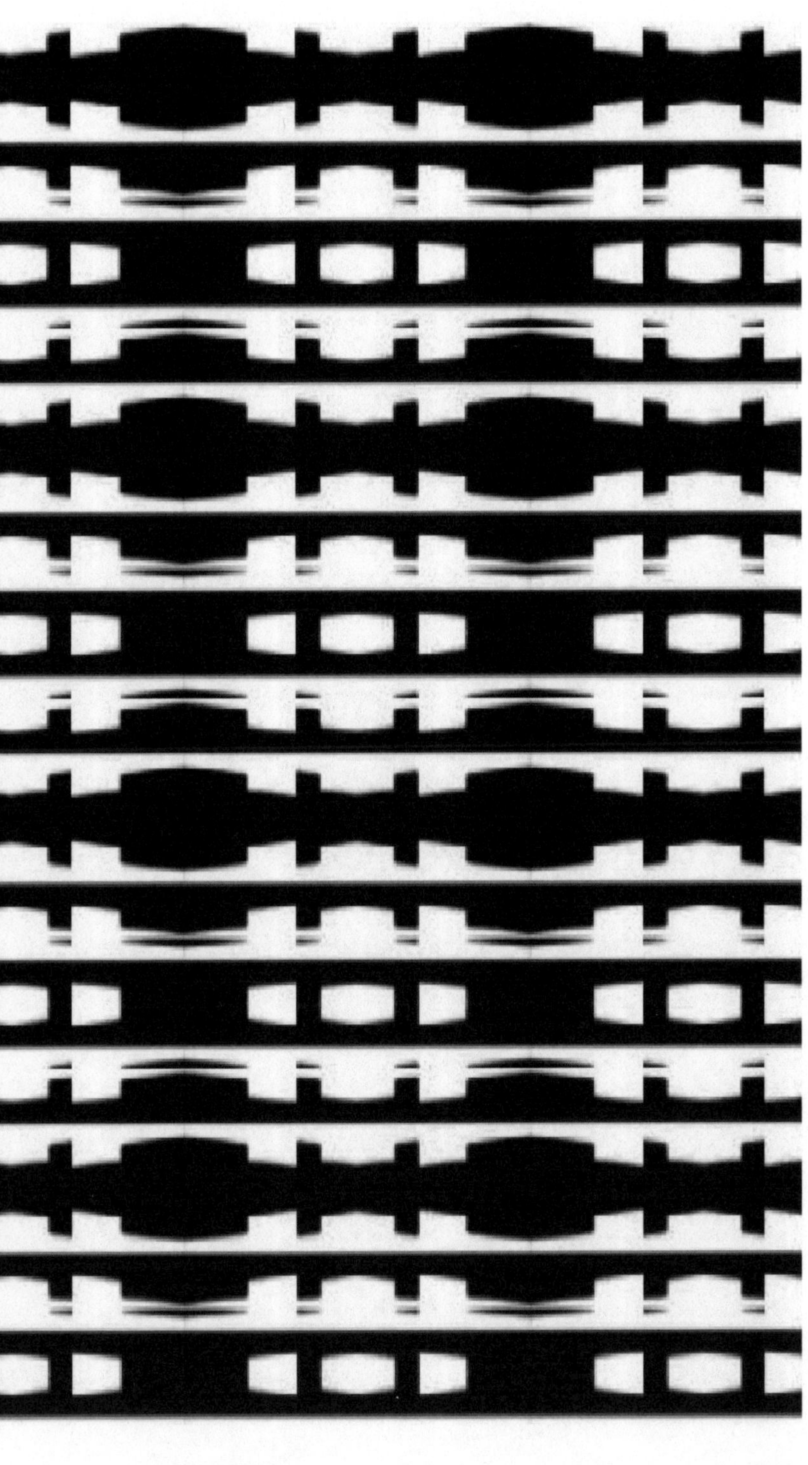

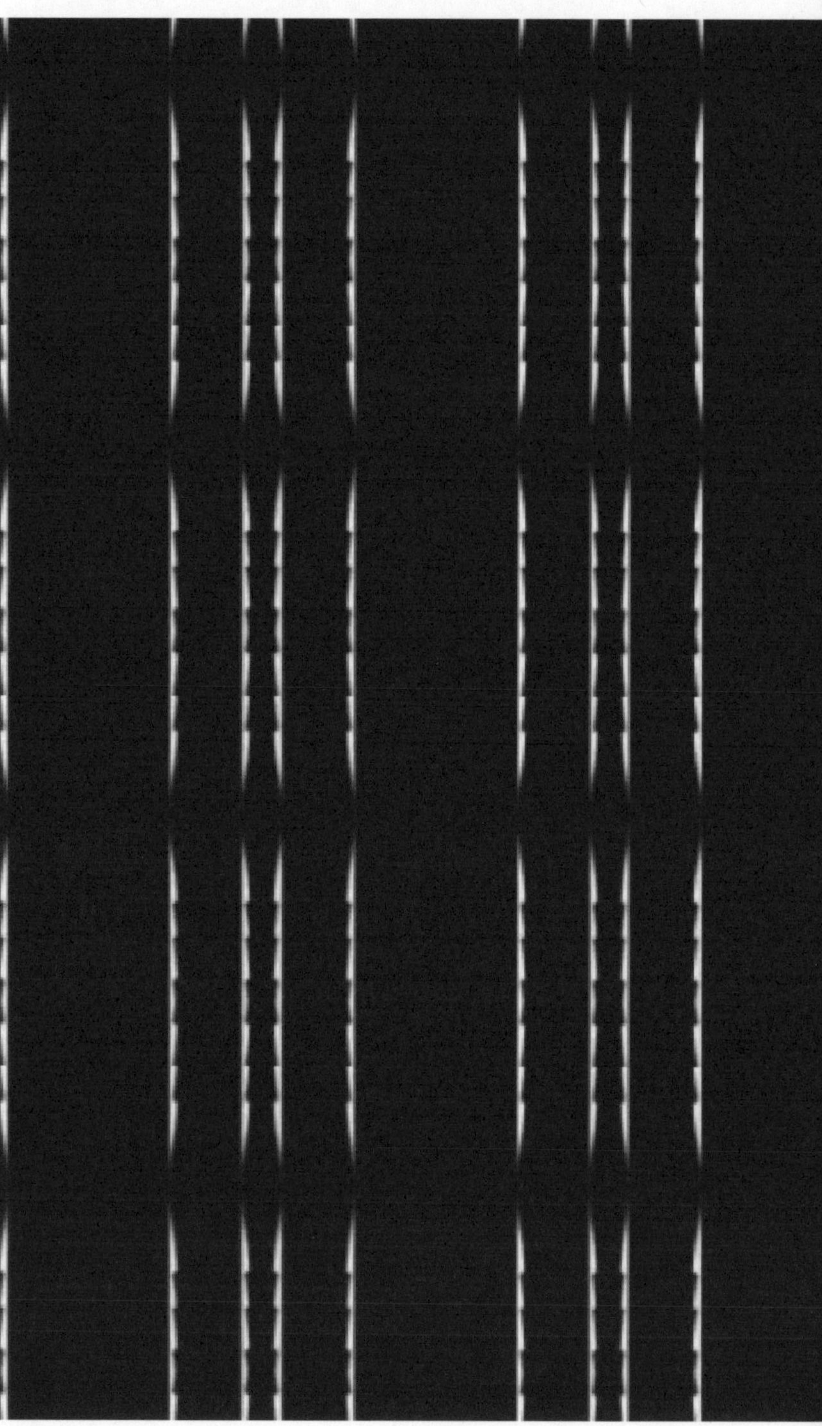

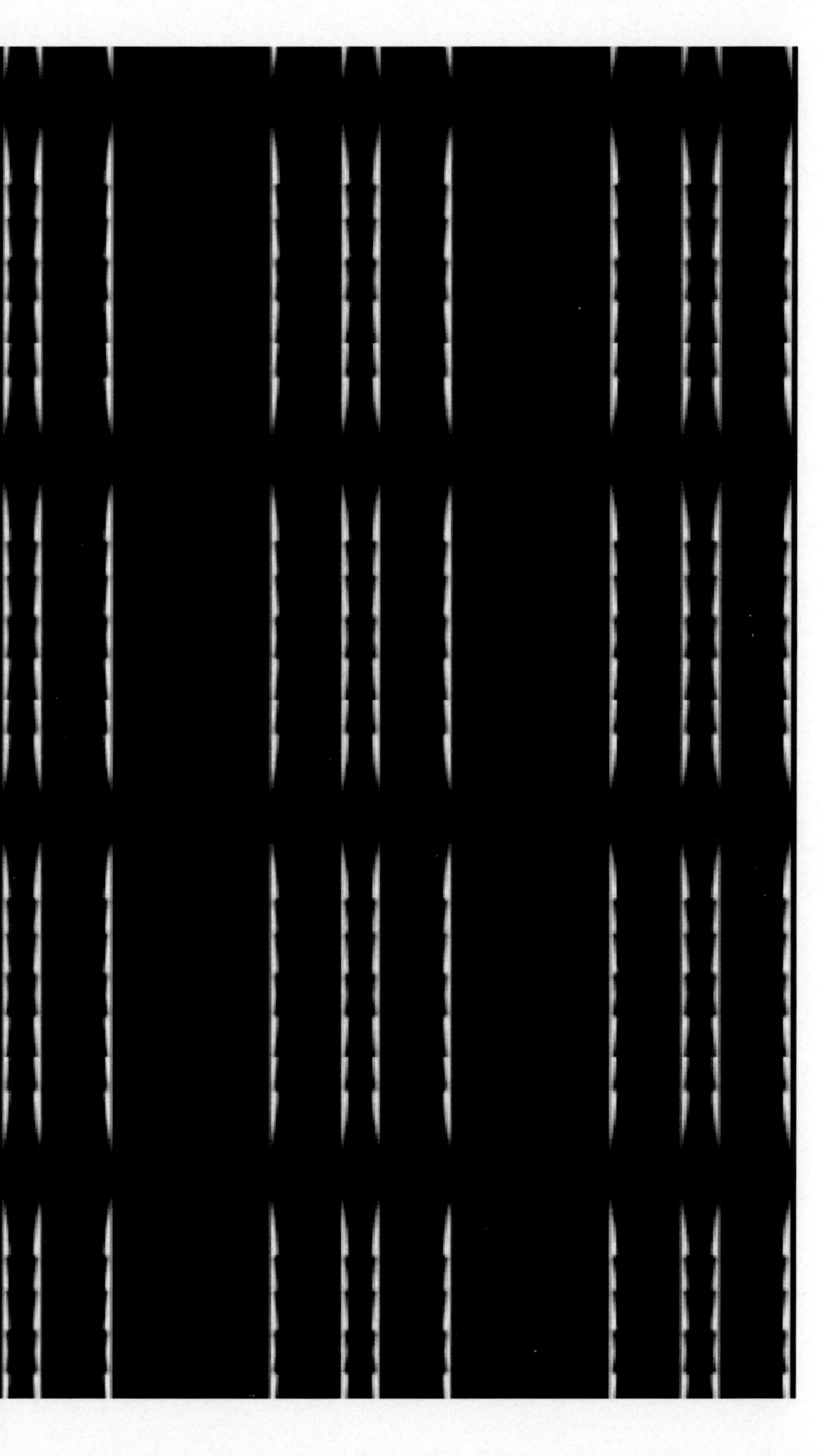

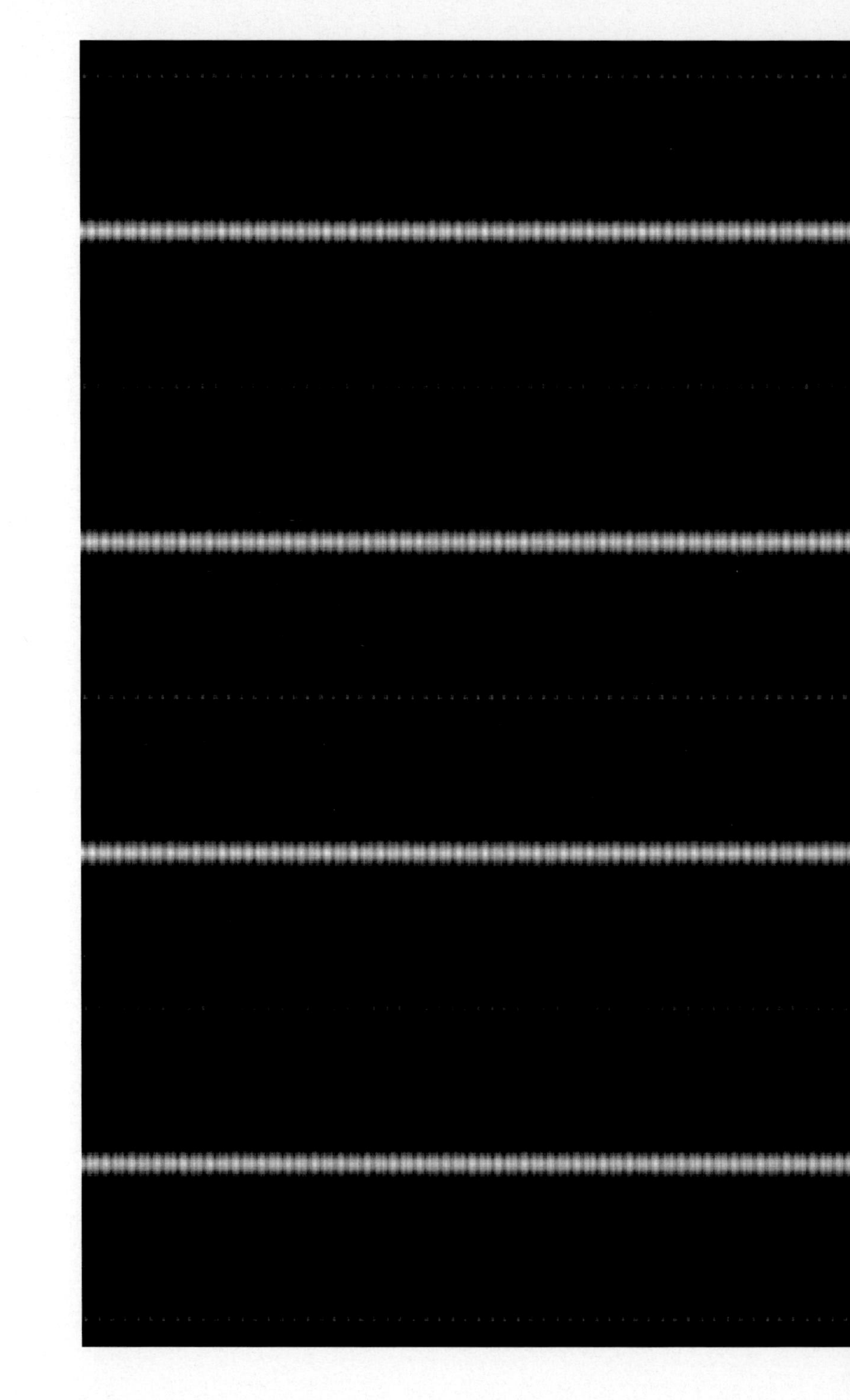

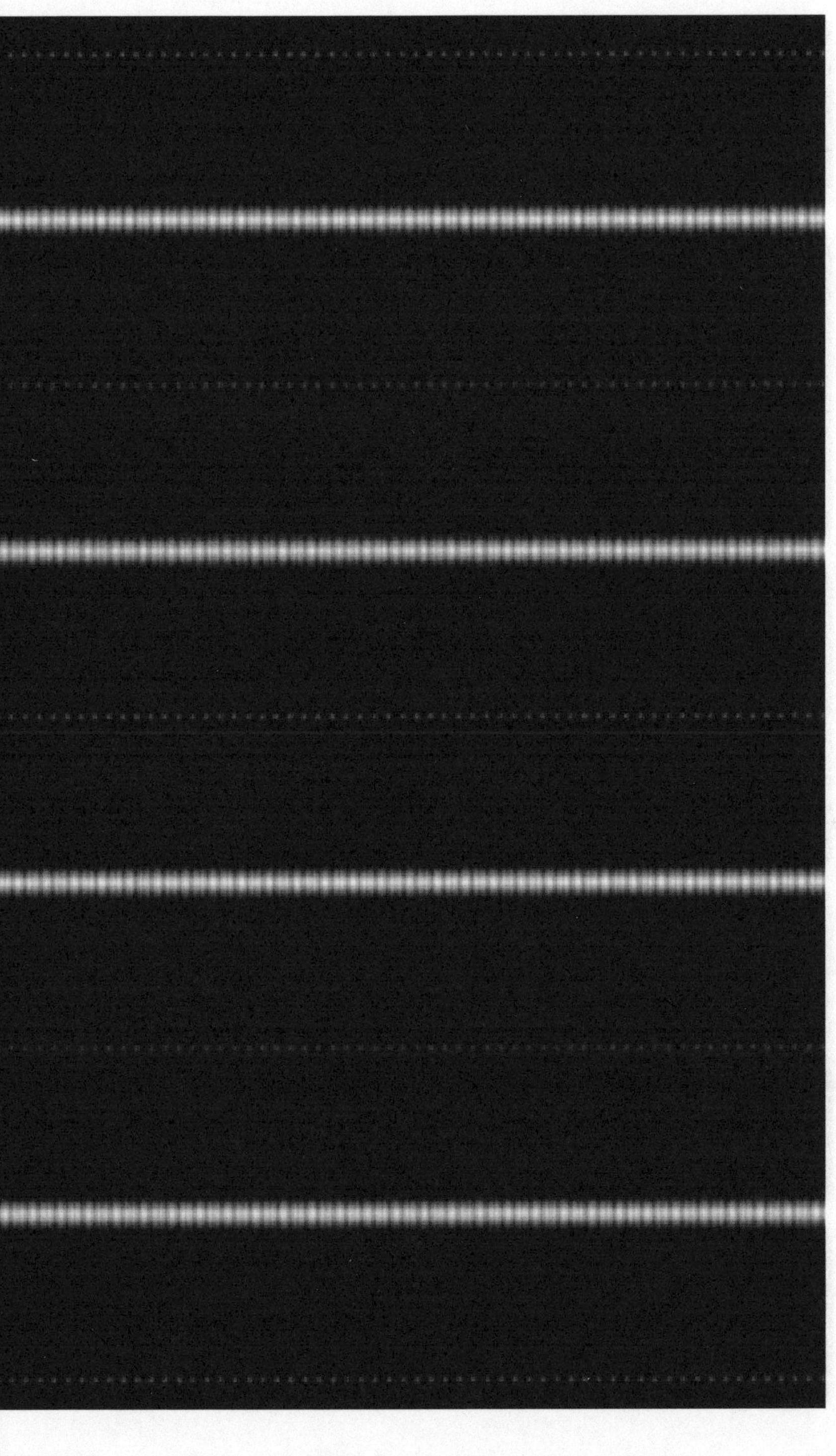

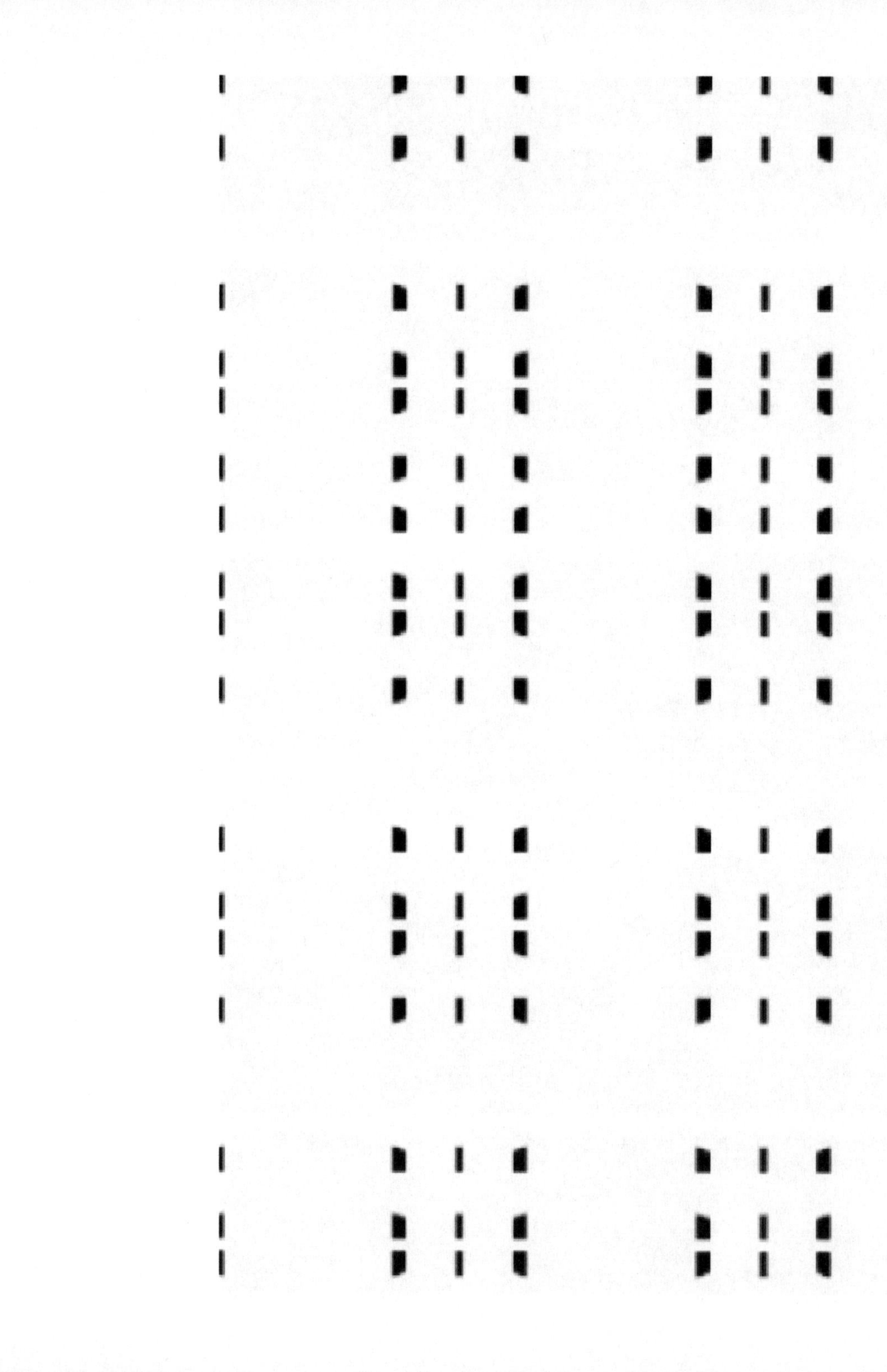

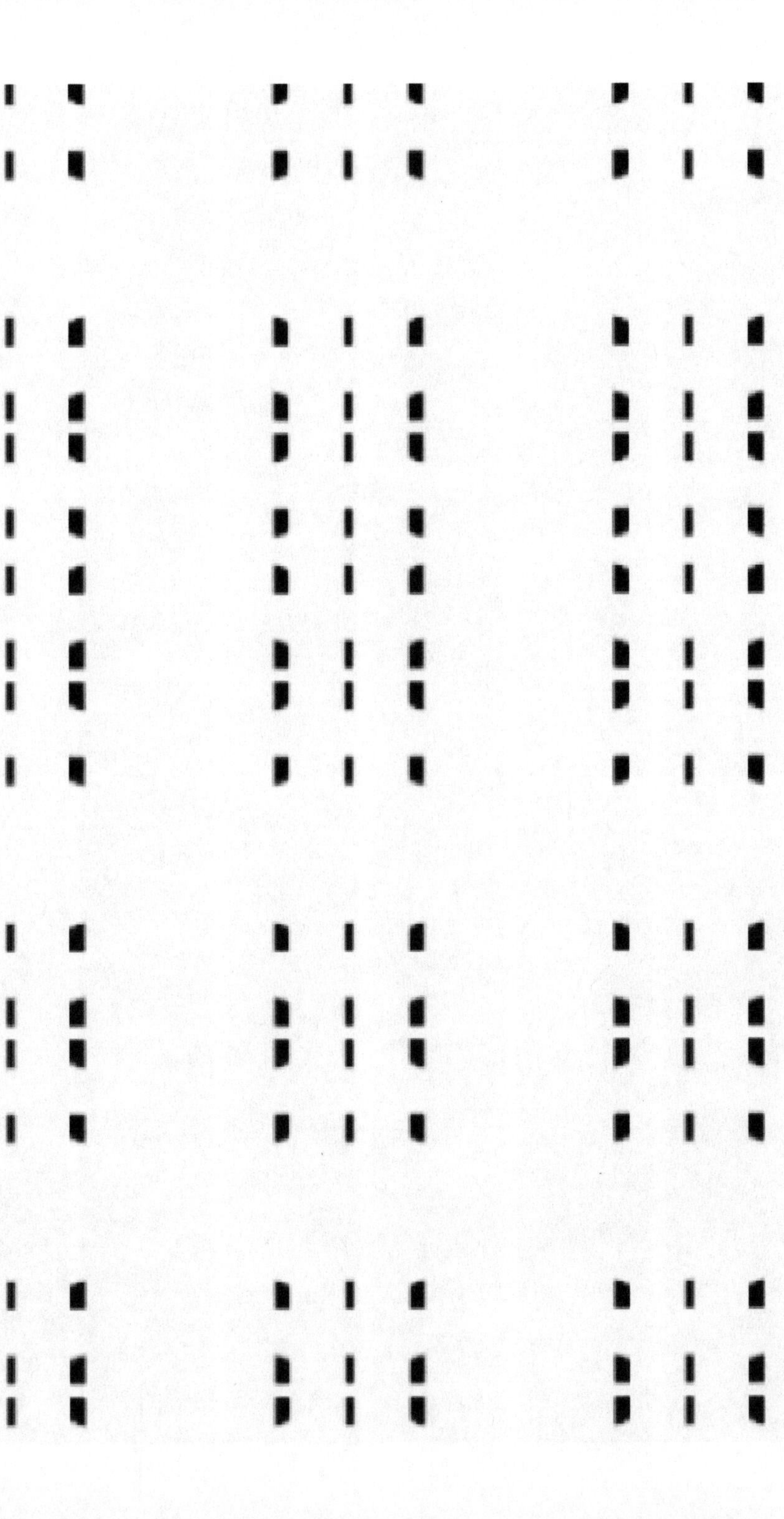

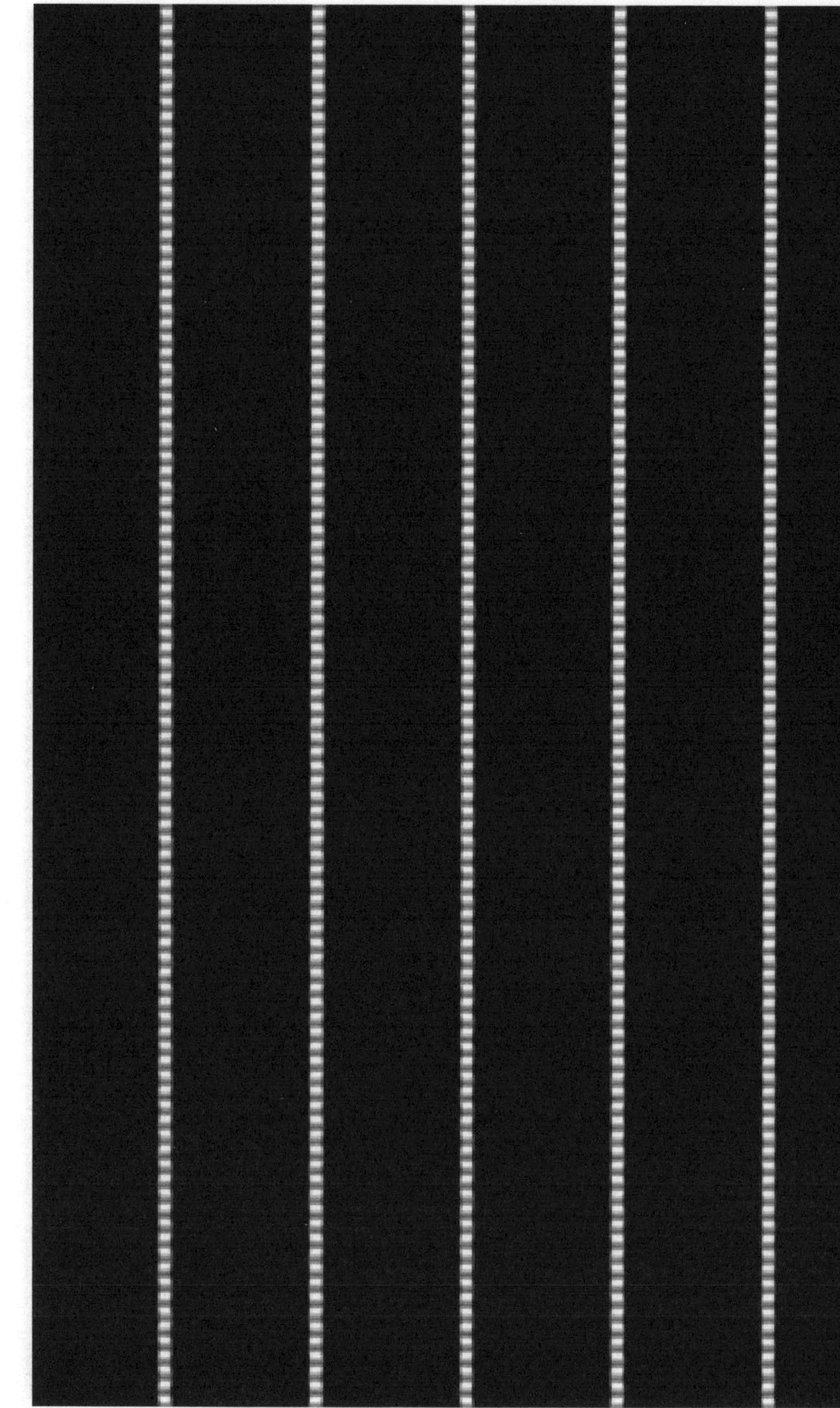

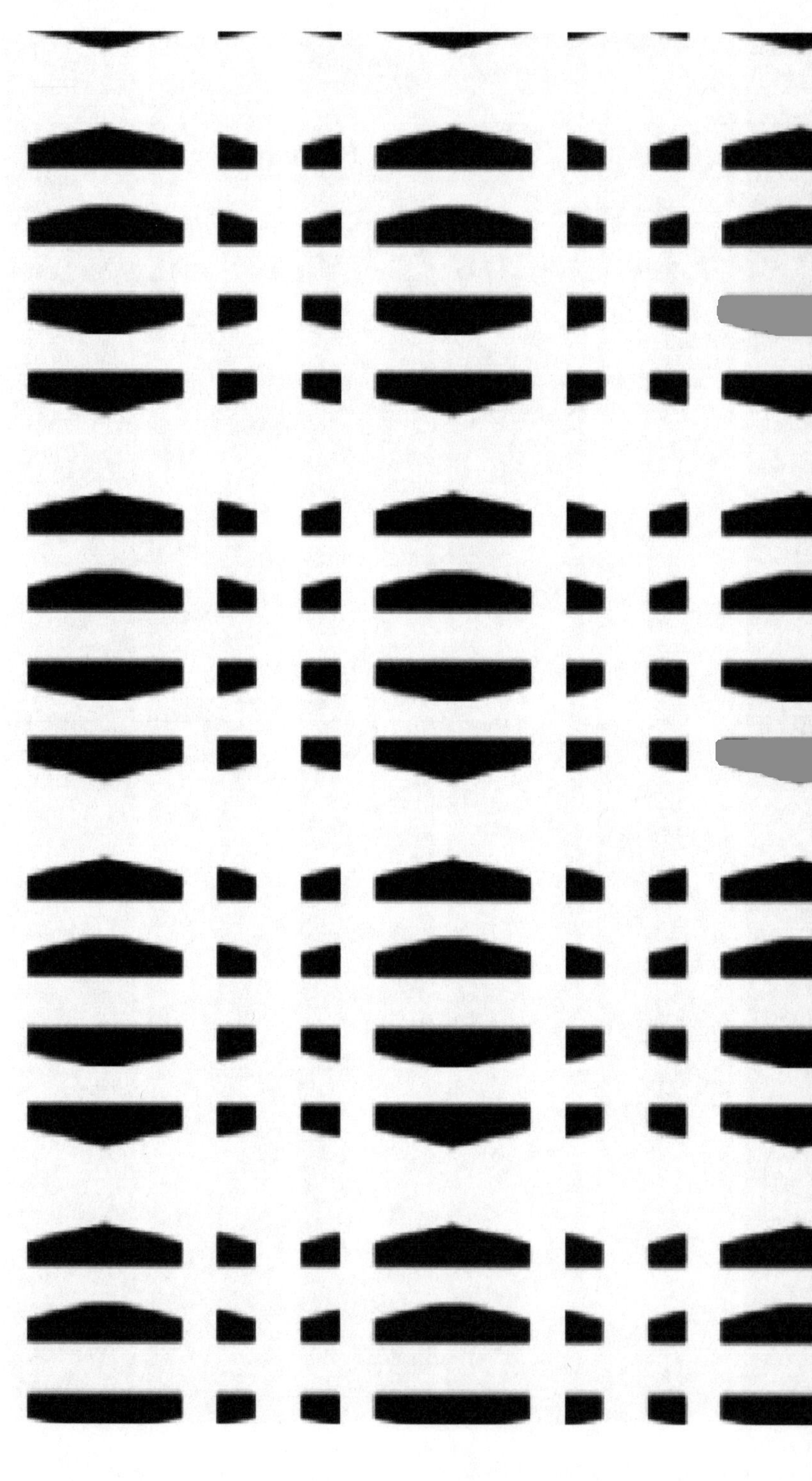

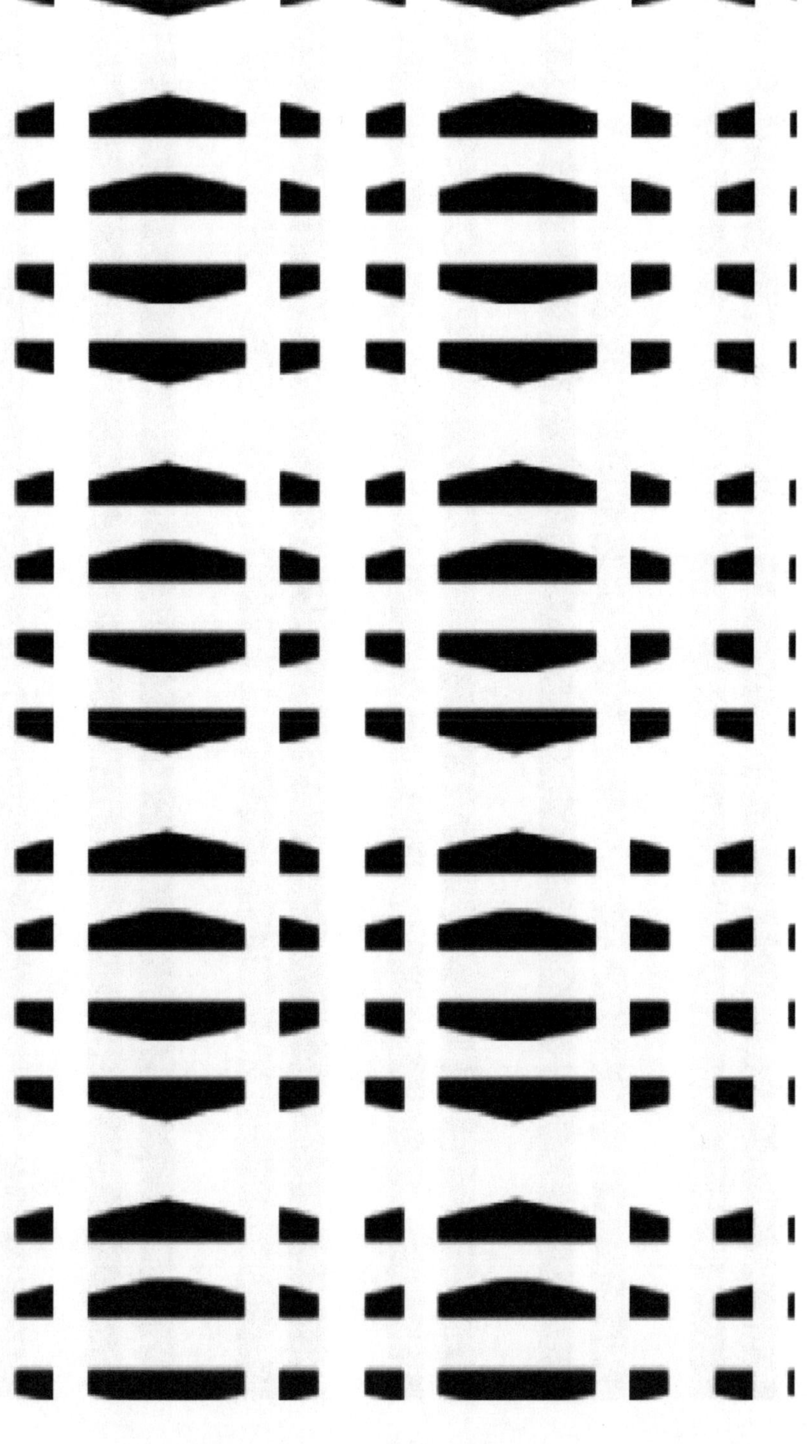

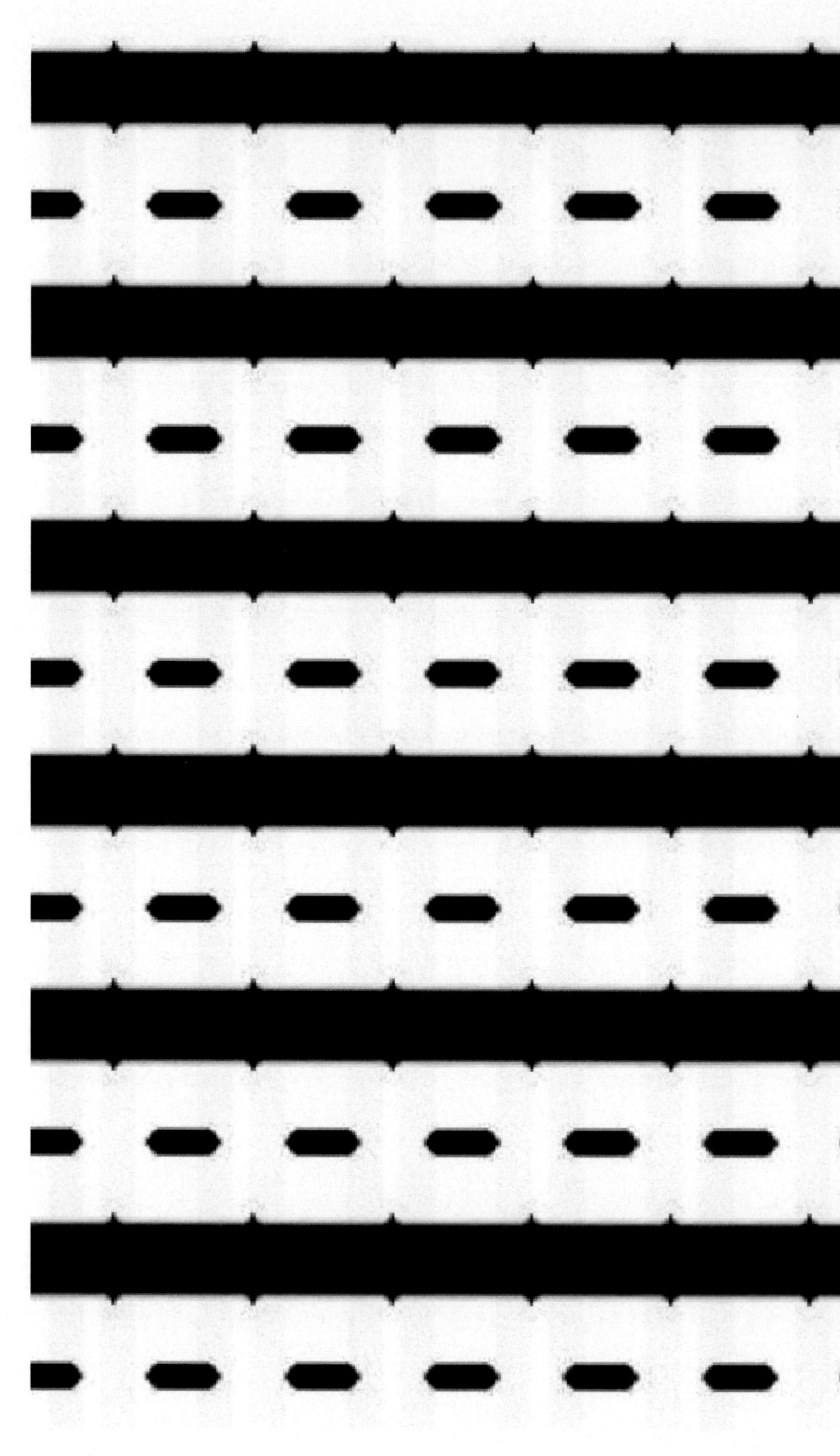

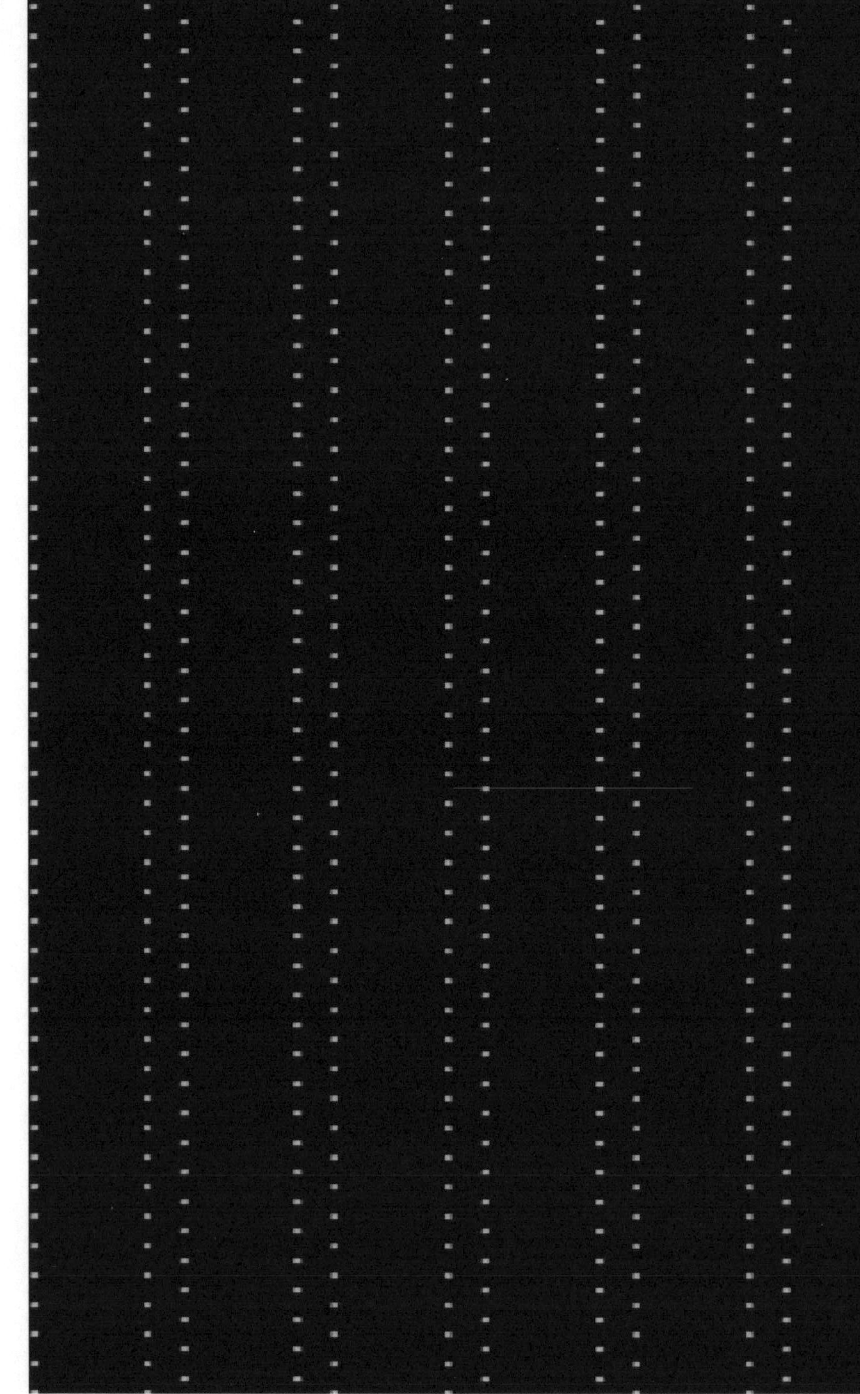

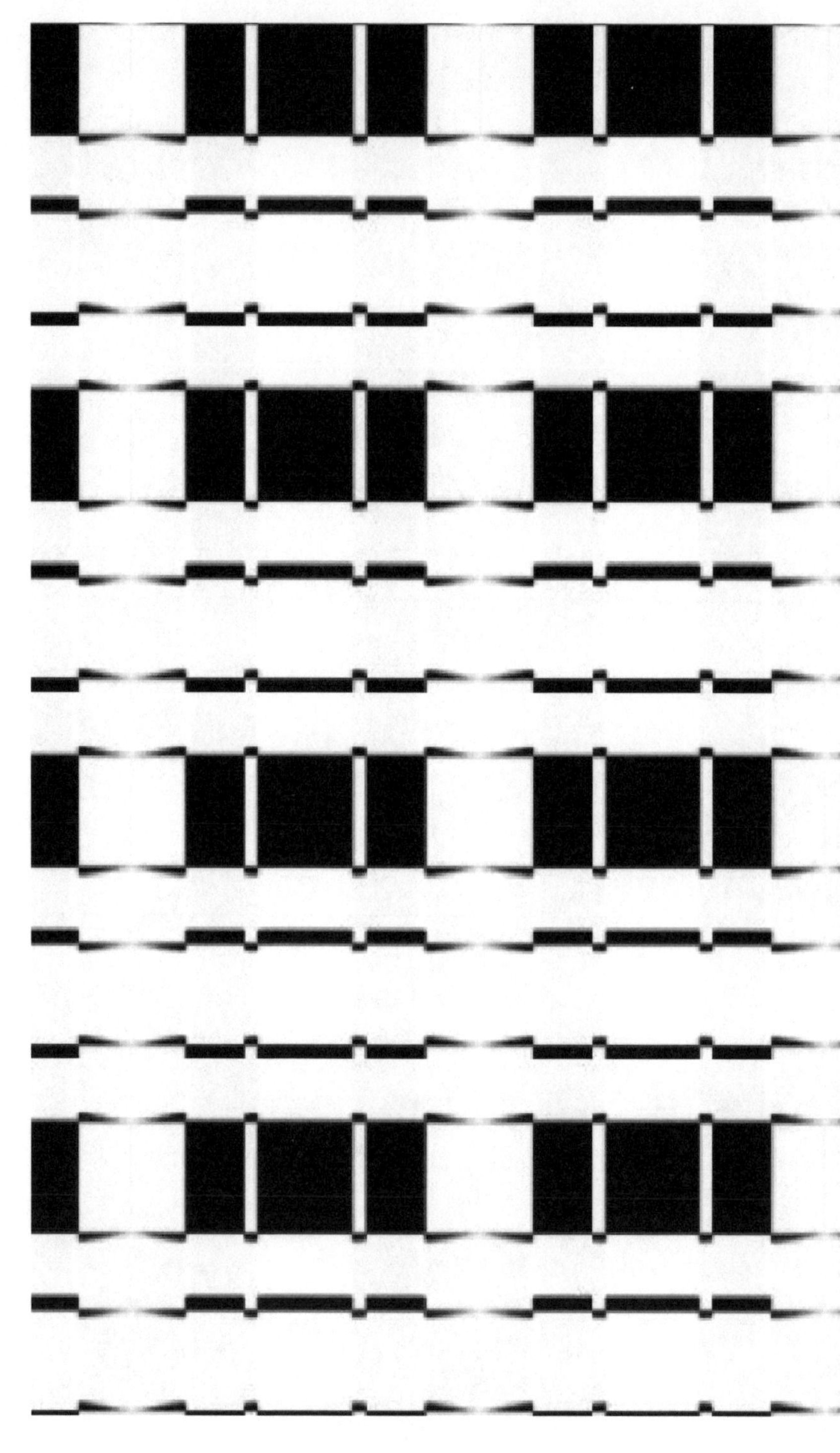

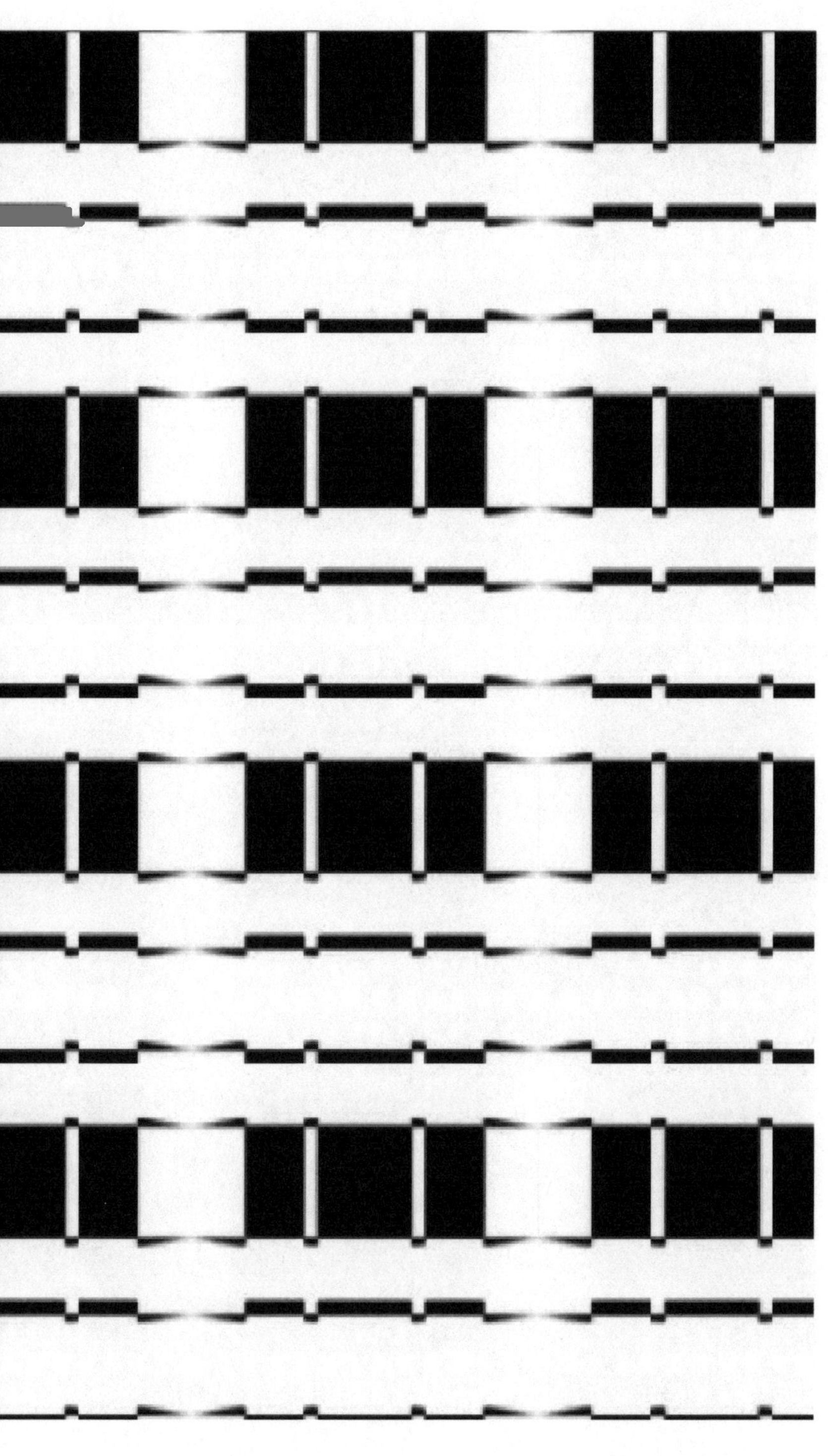

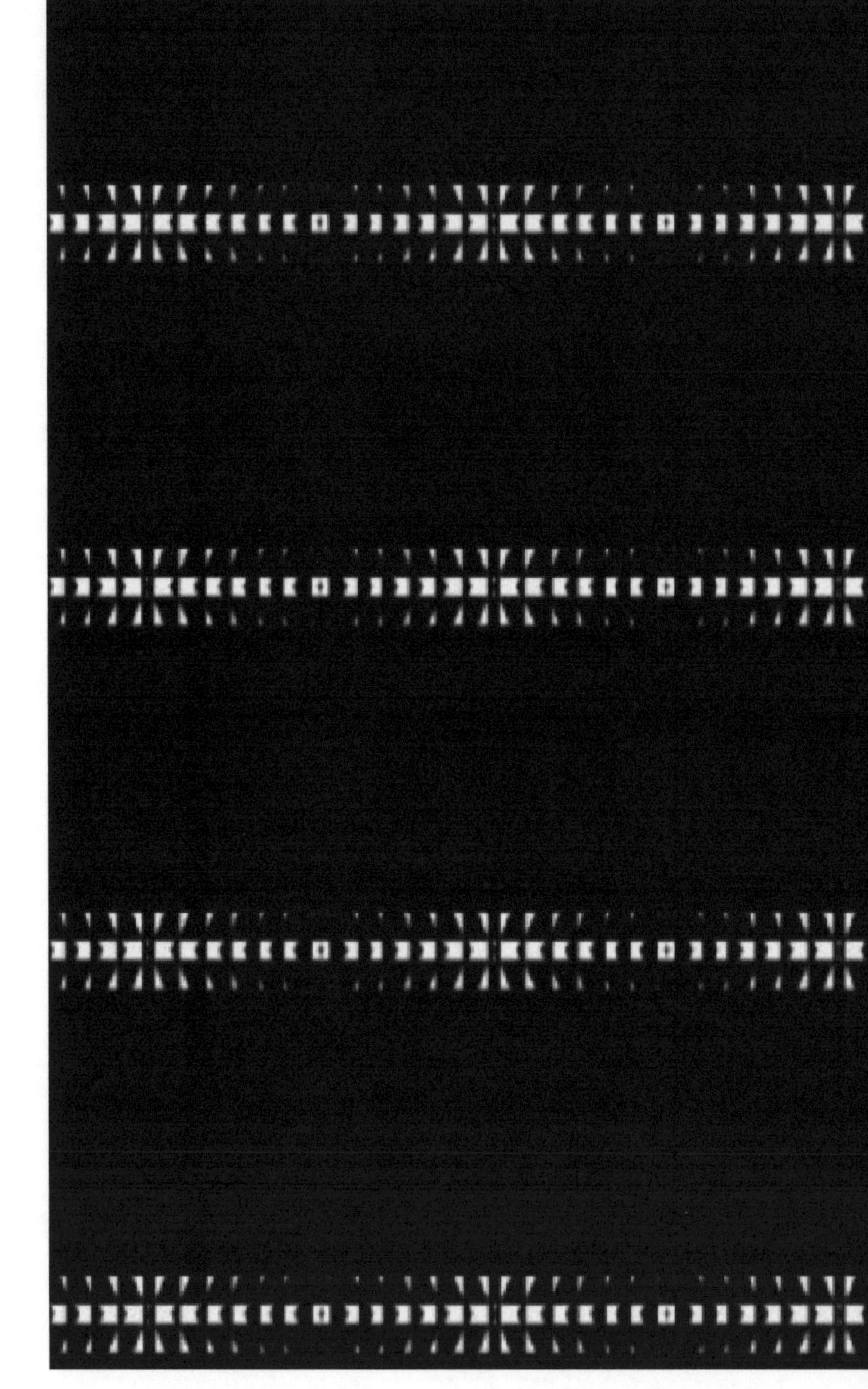

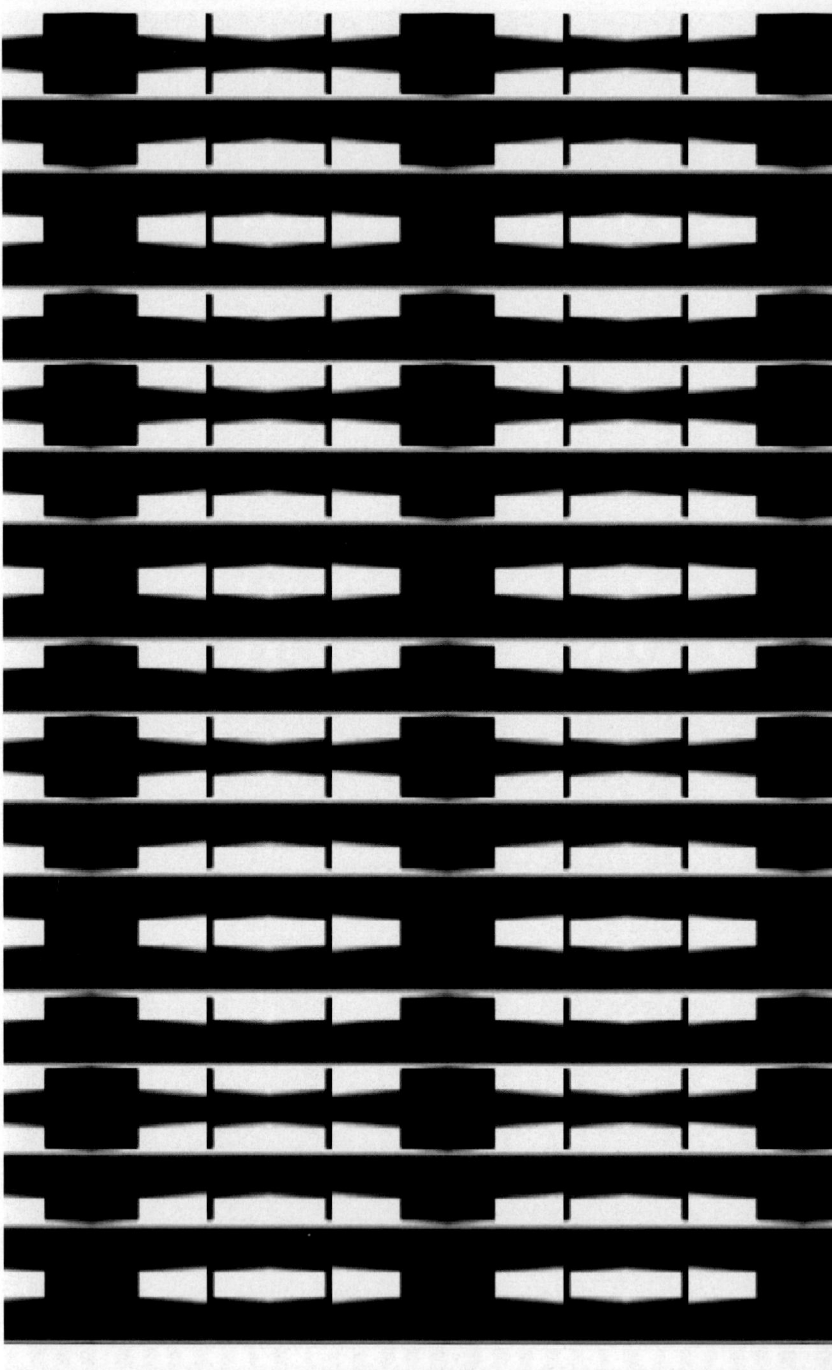

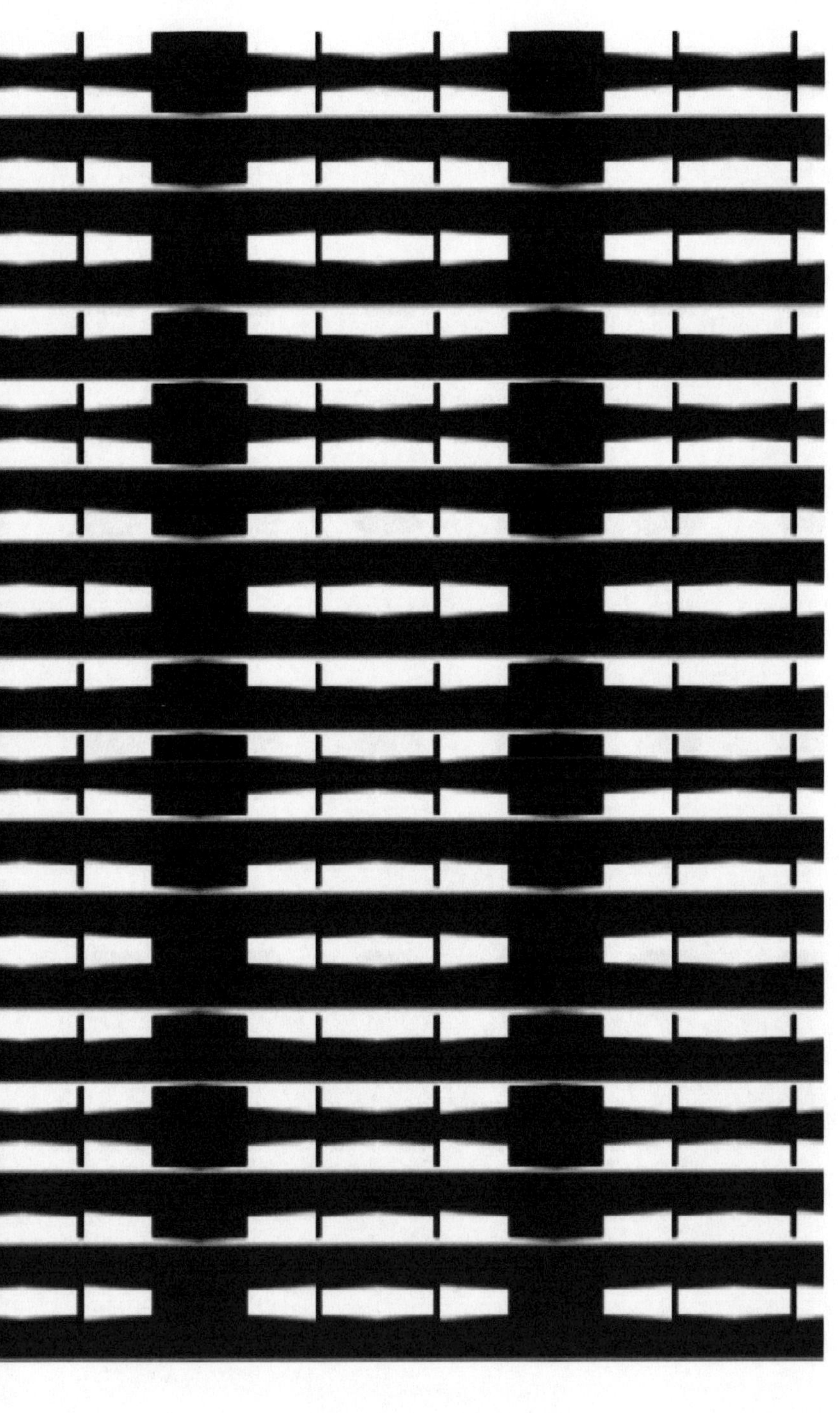

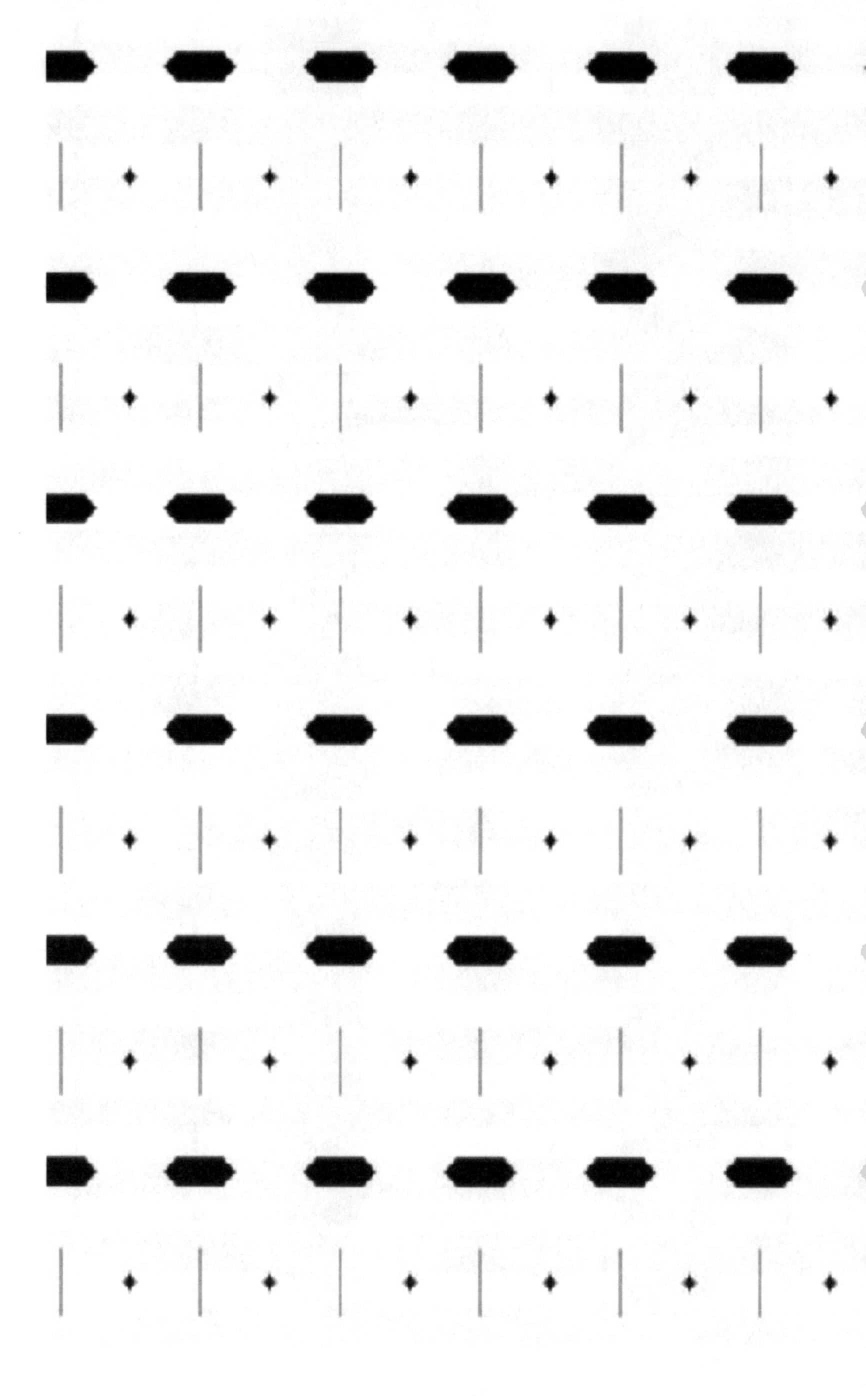

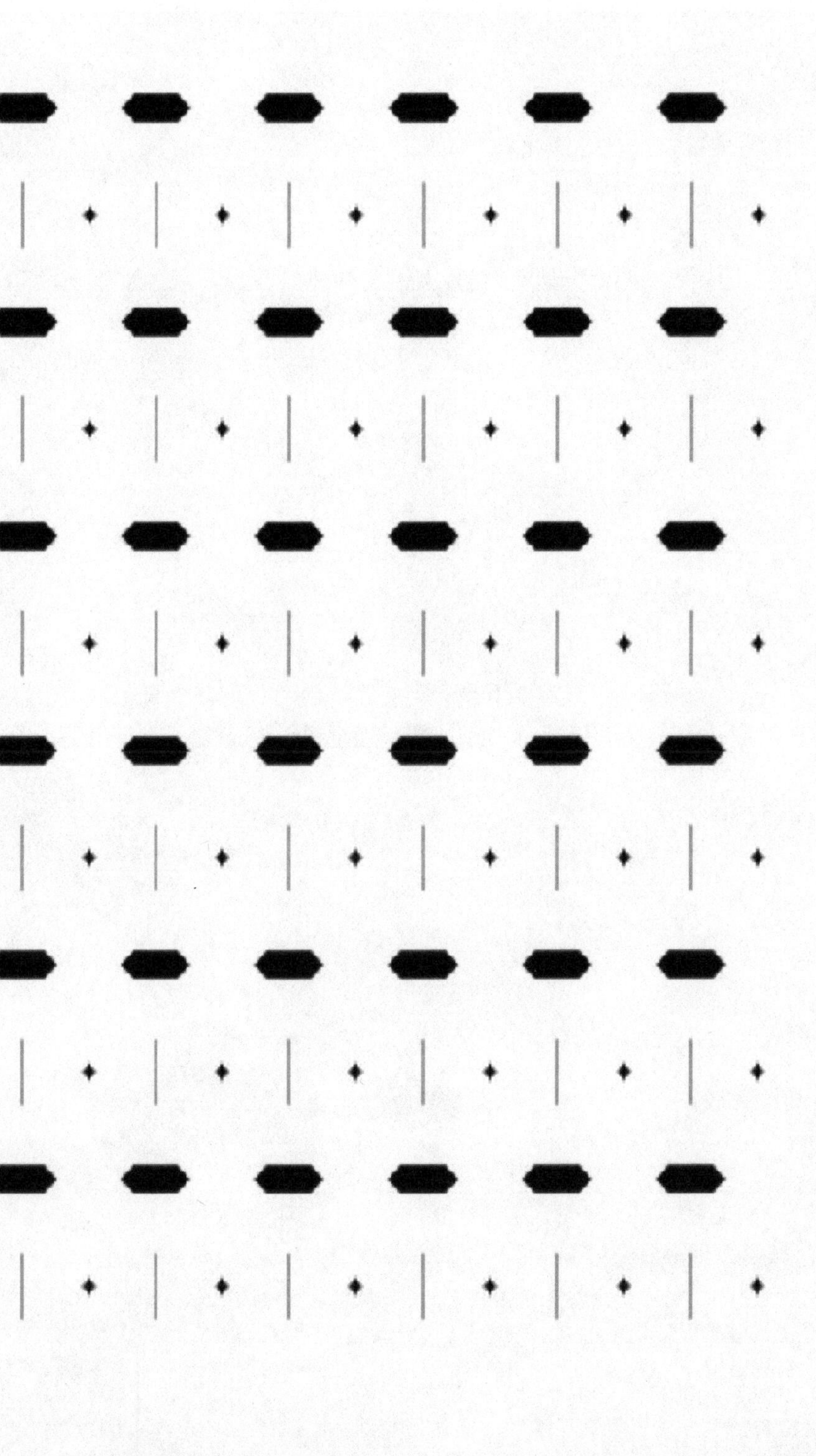

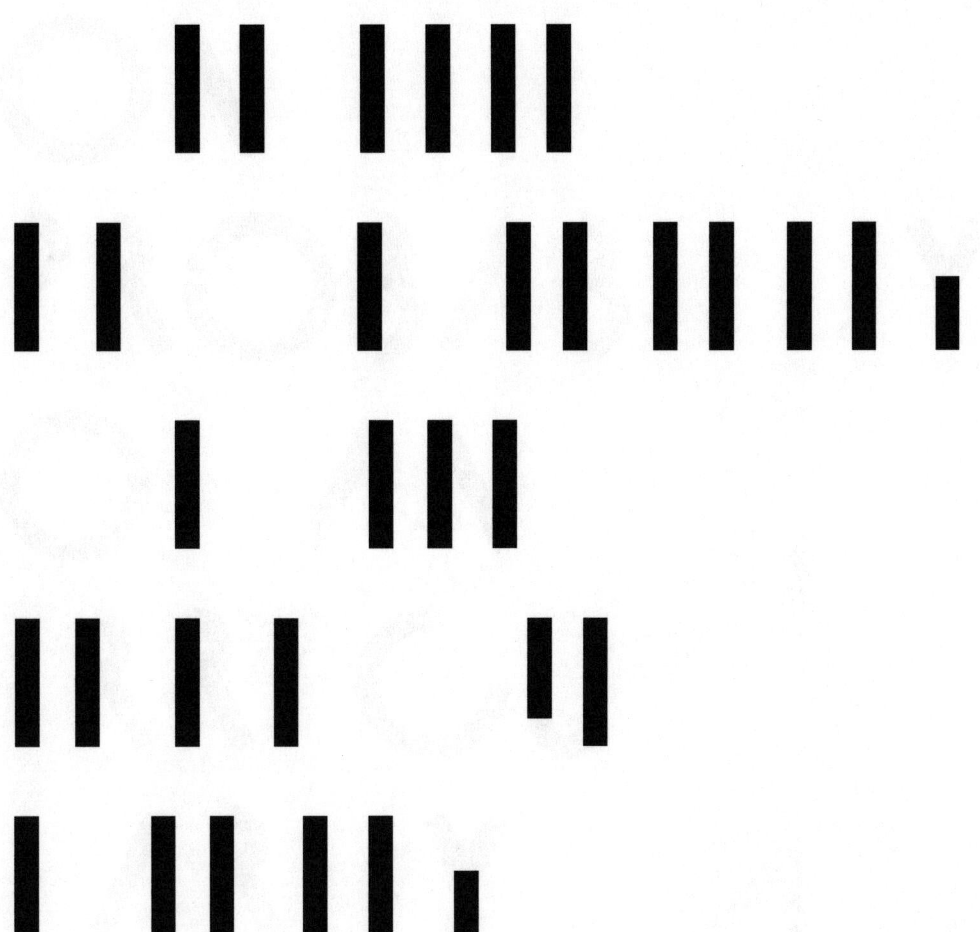

Aluminum, steel, air
compressors, solenoid
valves, electric motor,
micro switches, confetti
150 x 150 x 100 cm

2010

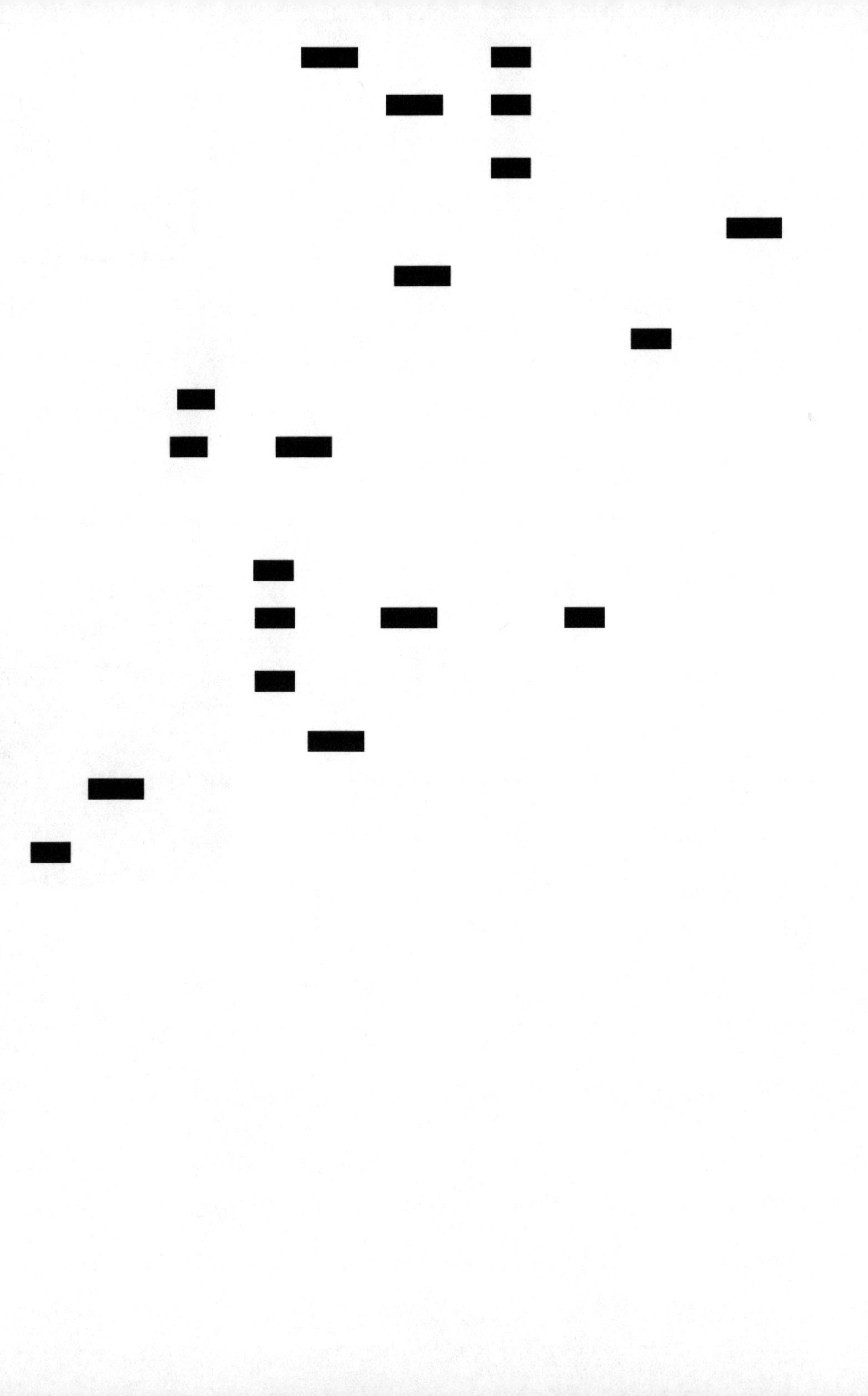

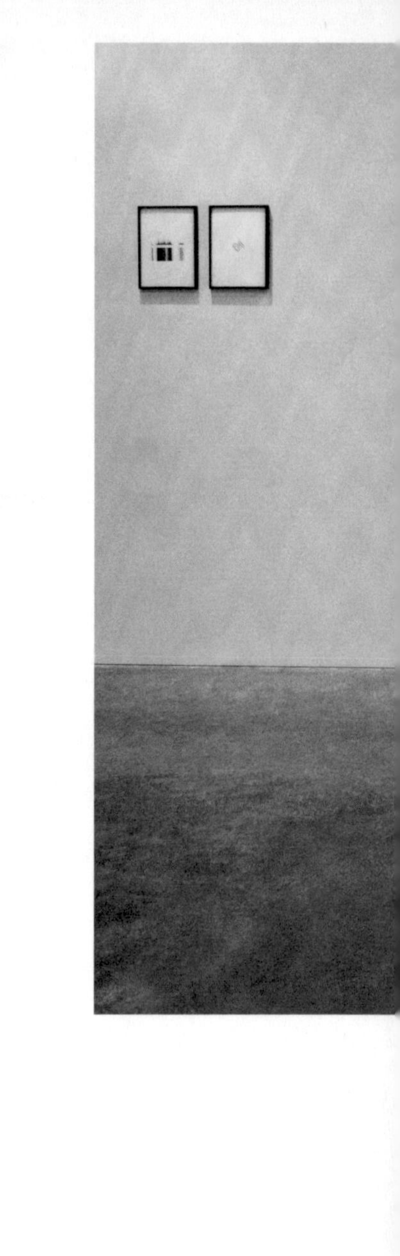

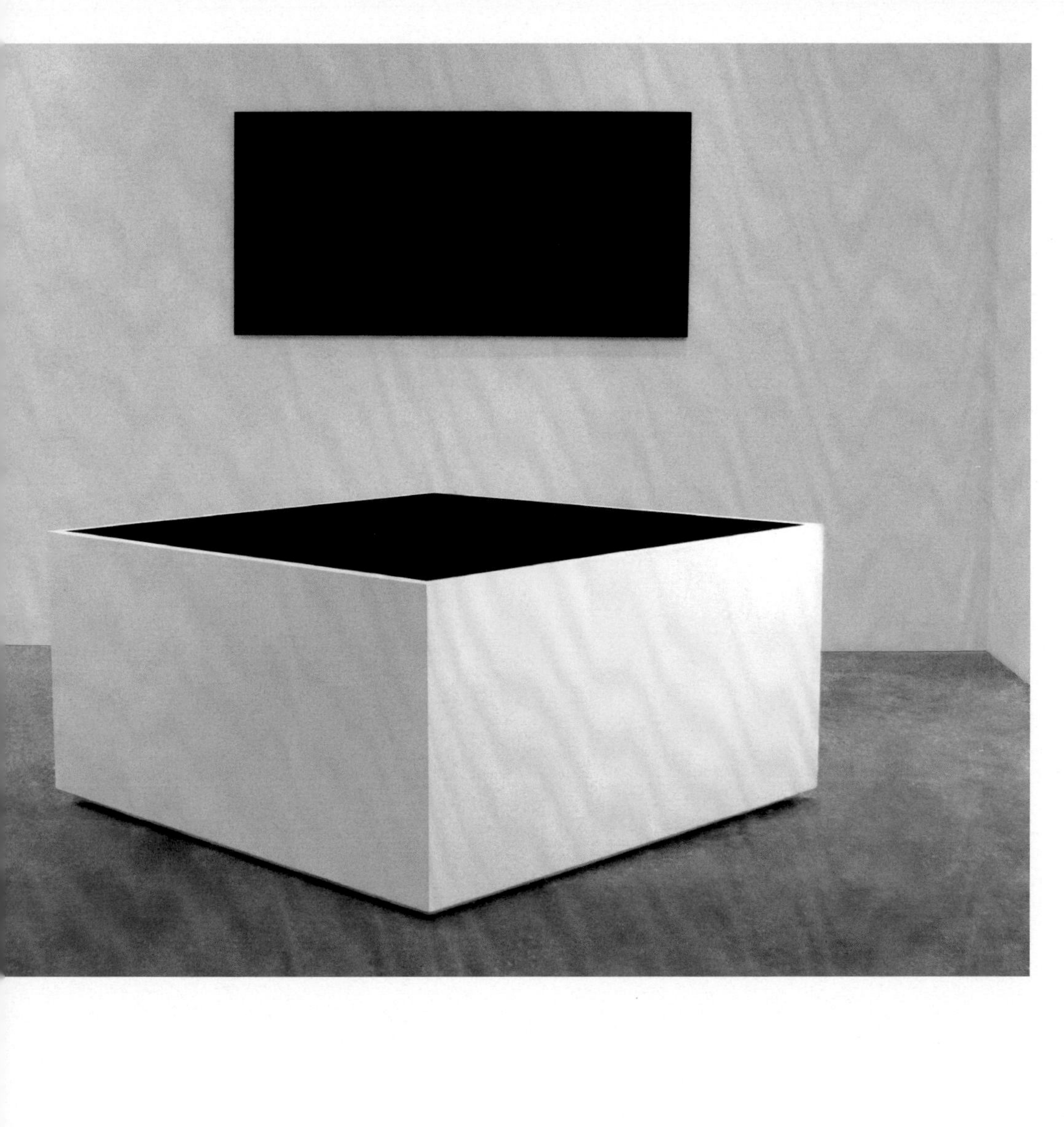

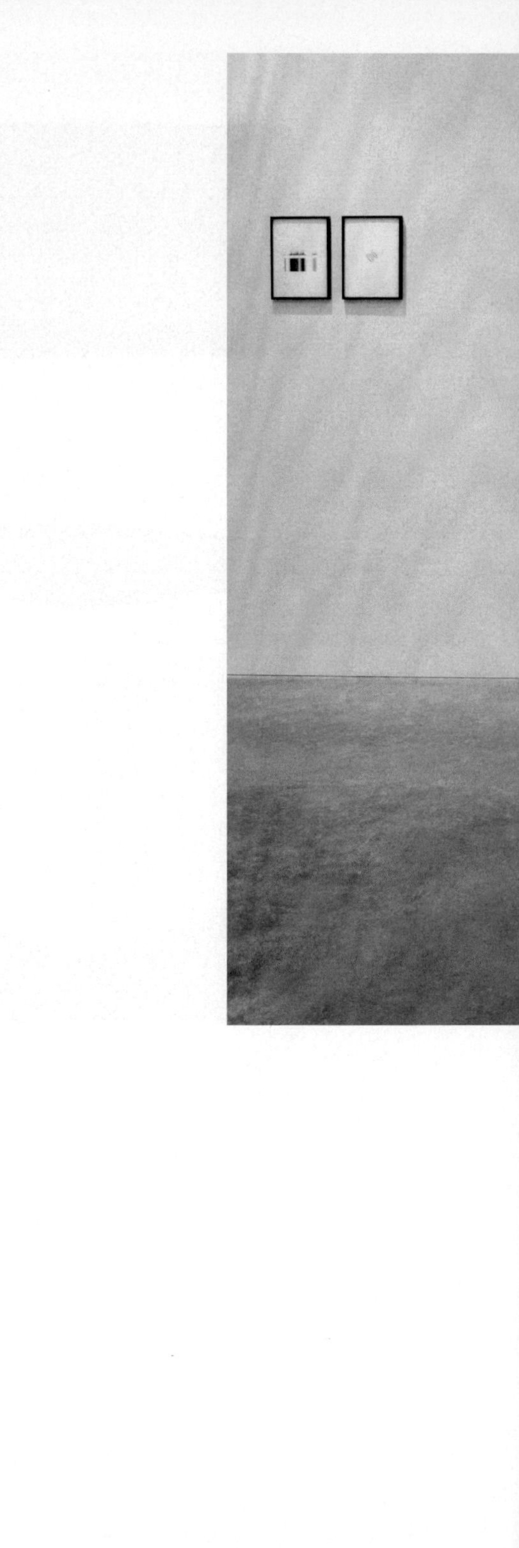

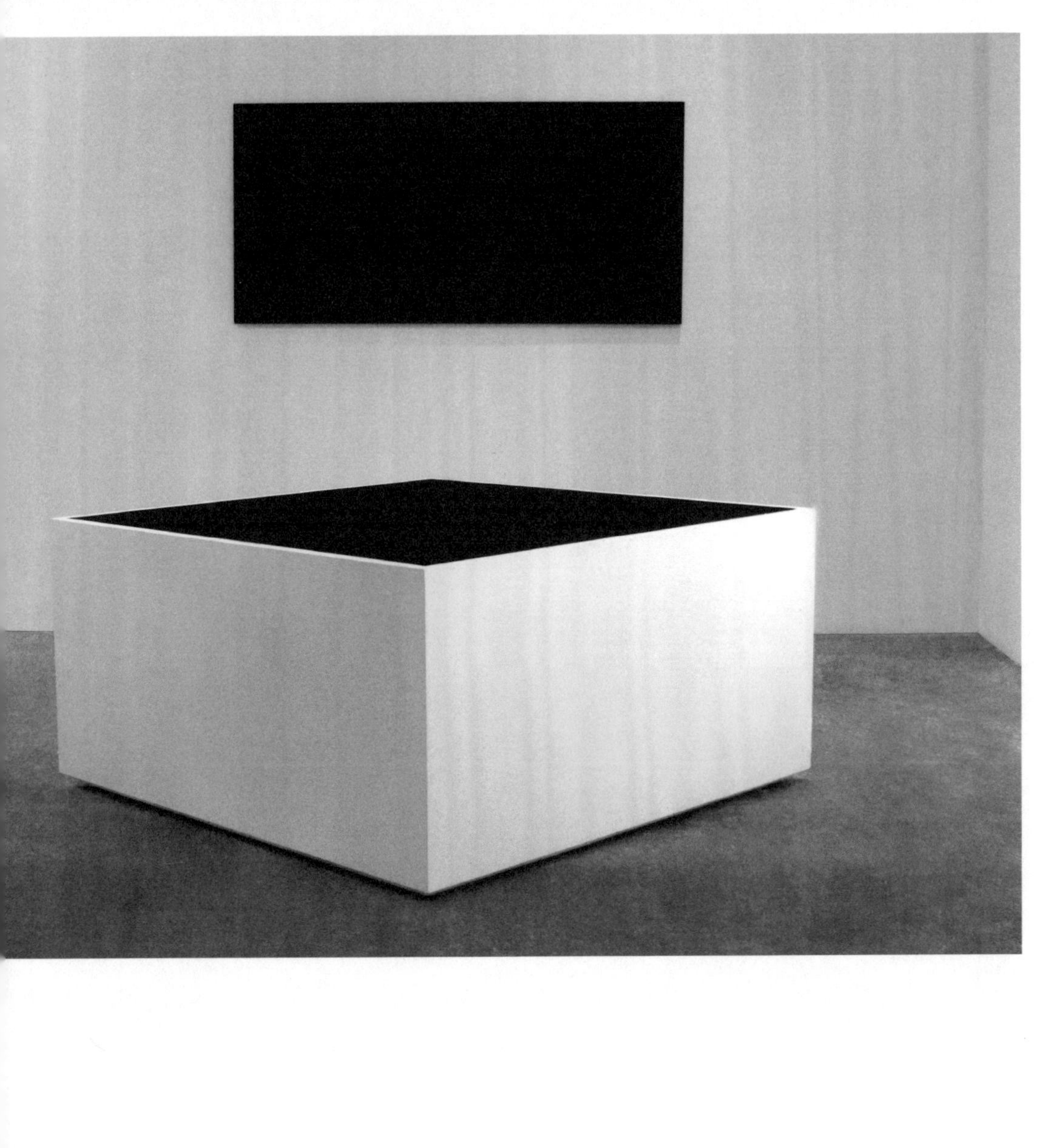

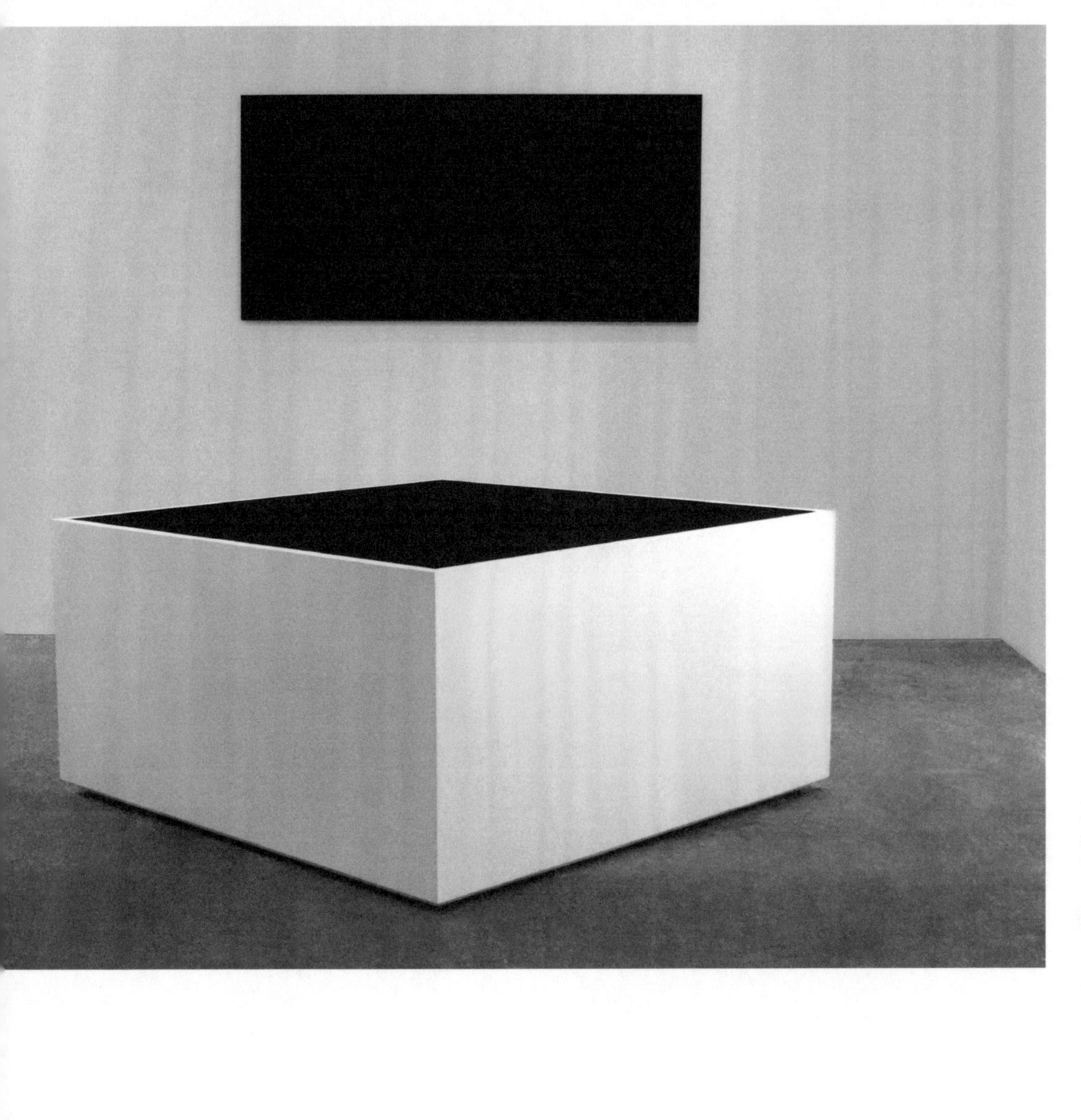

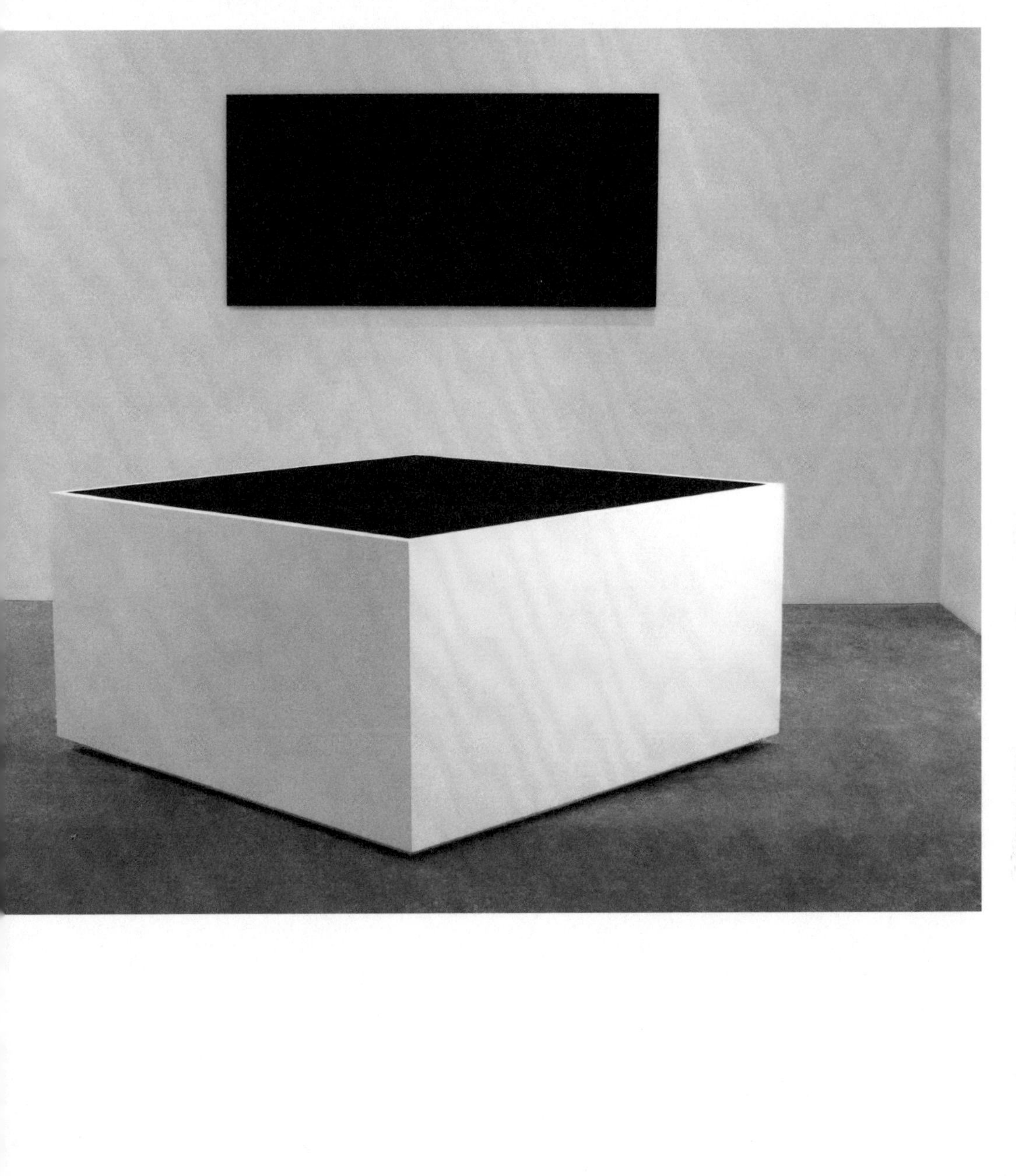

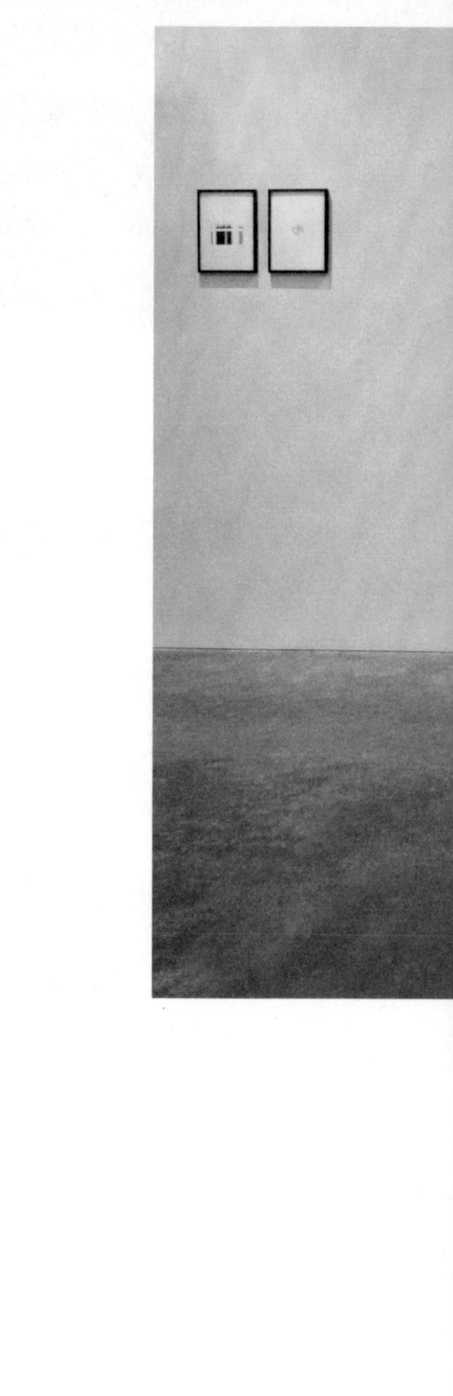

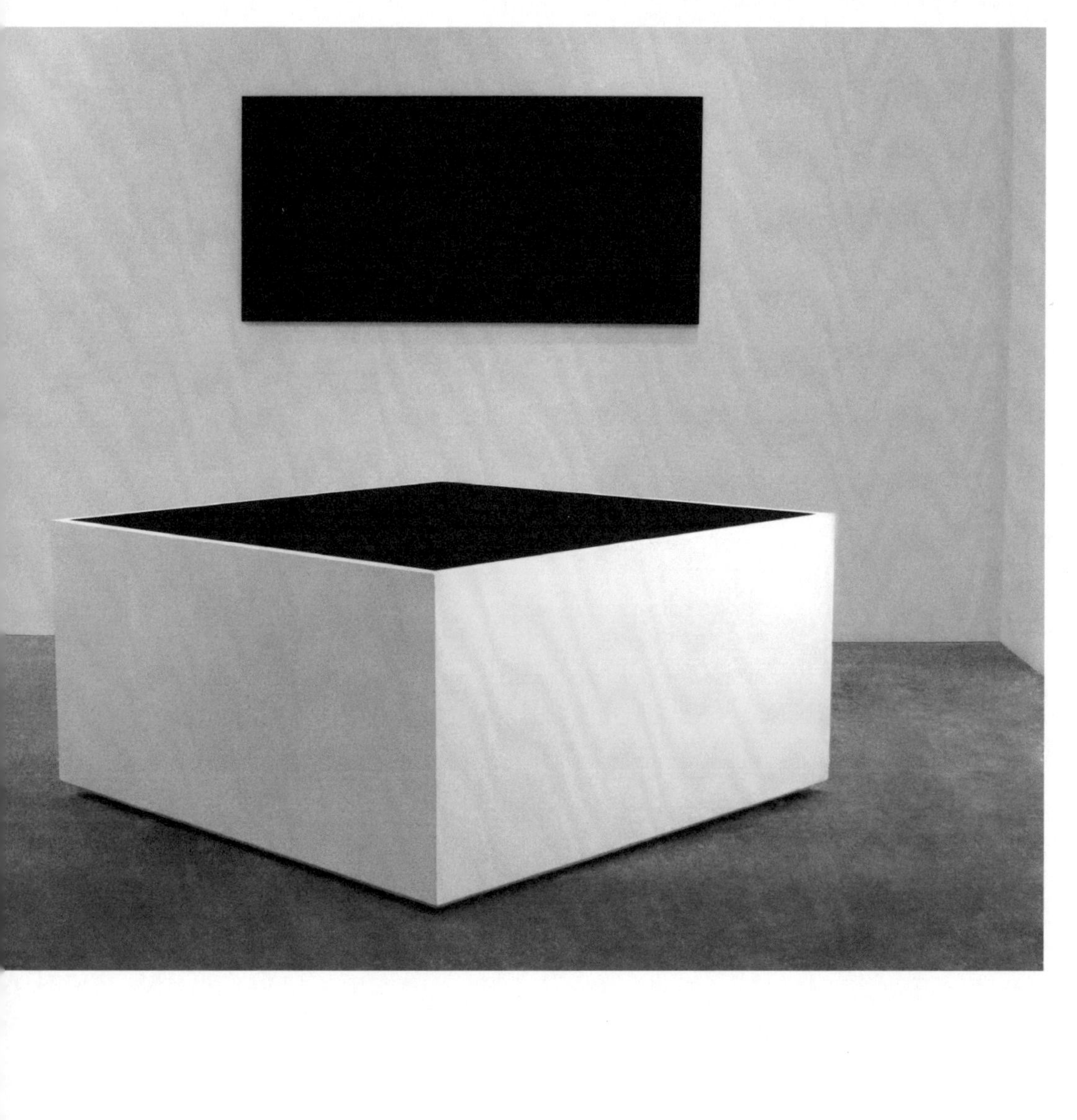

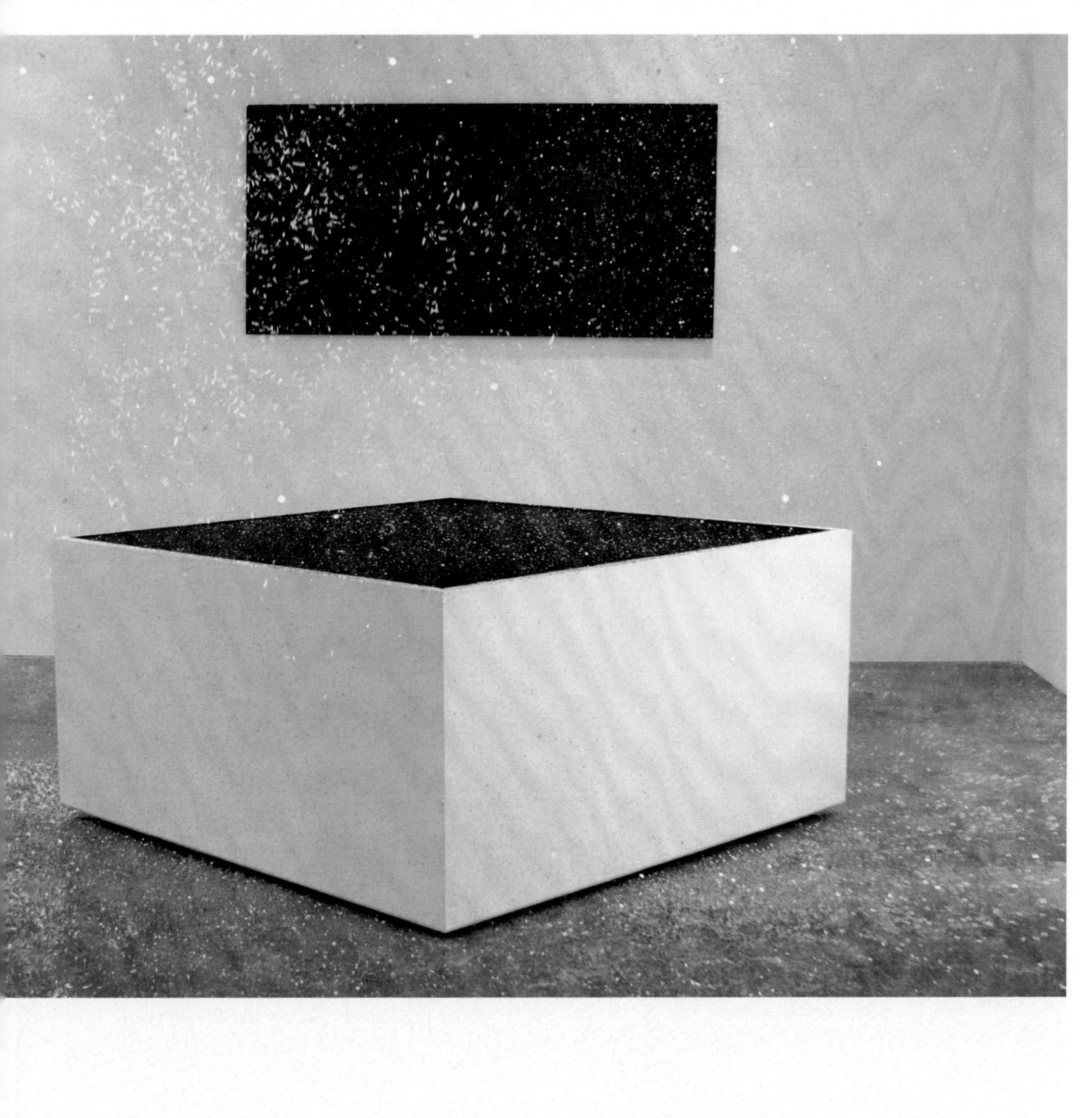

2007

HD video projection,
color, no sound, 4 mins

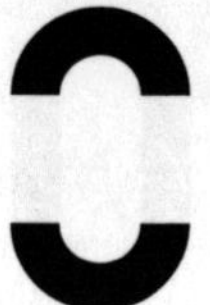

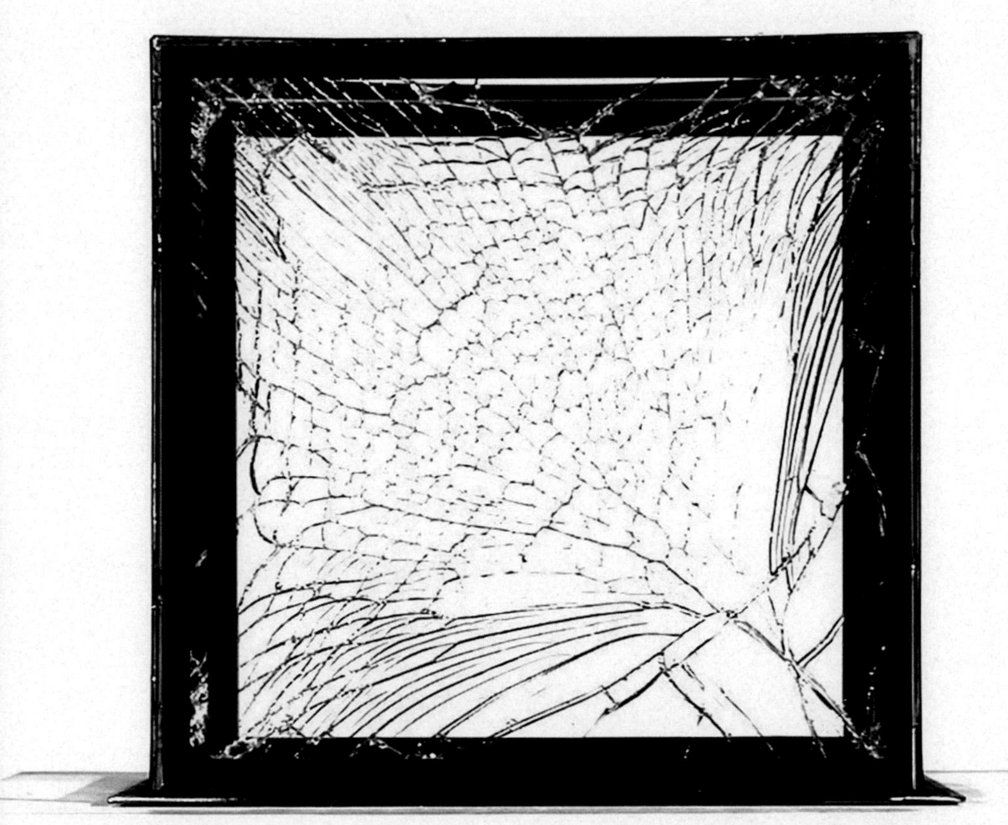

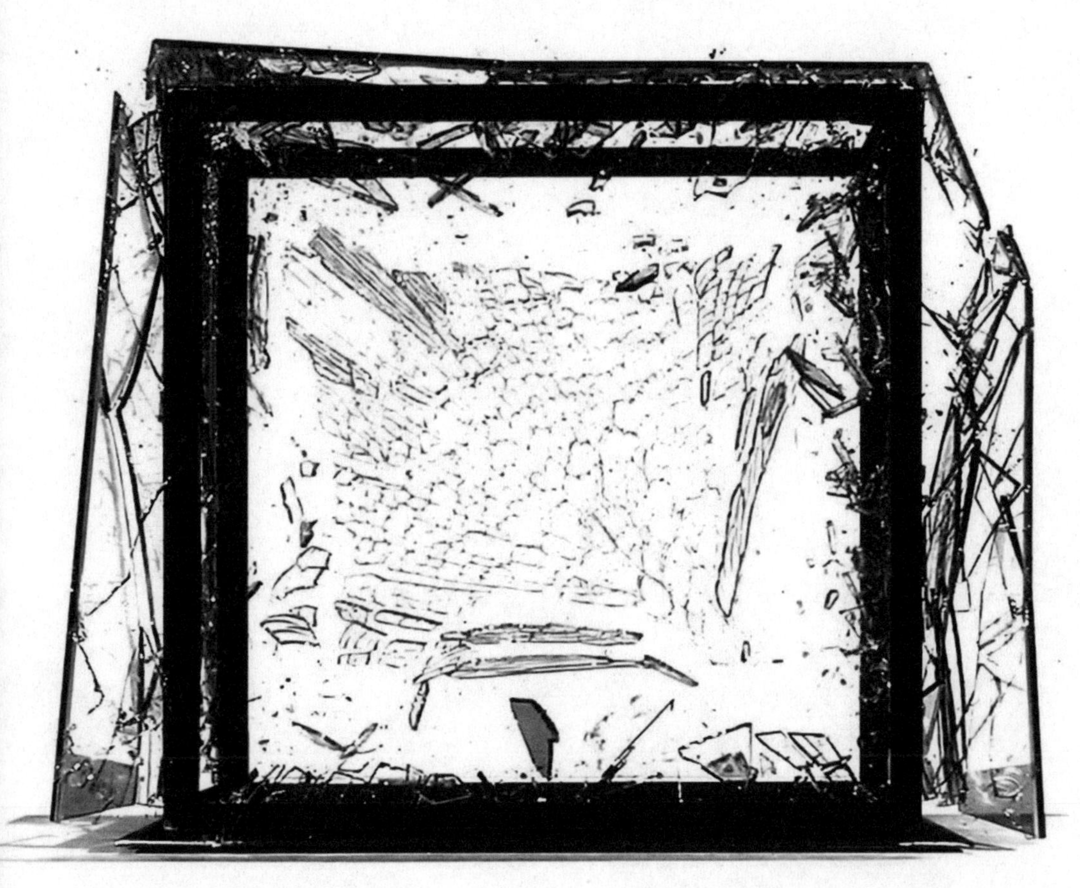

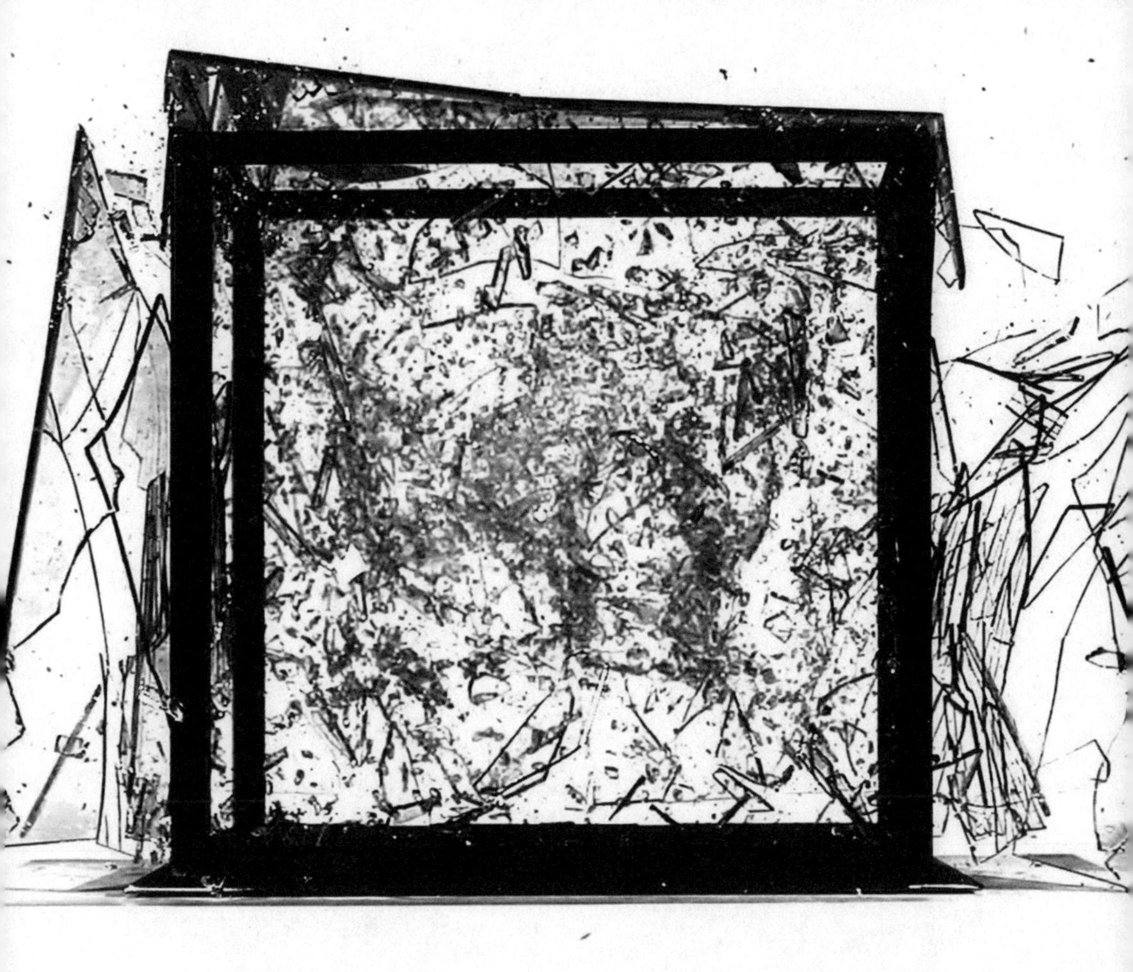

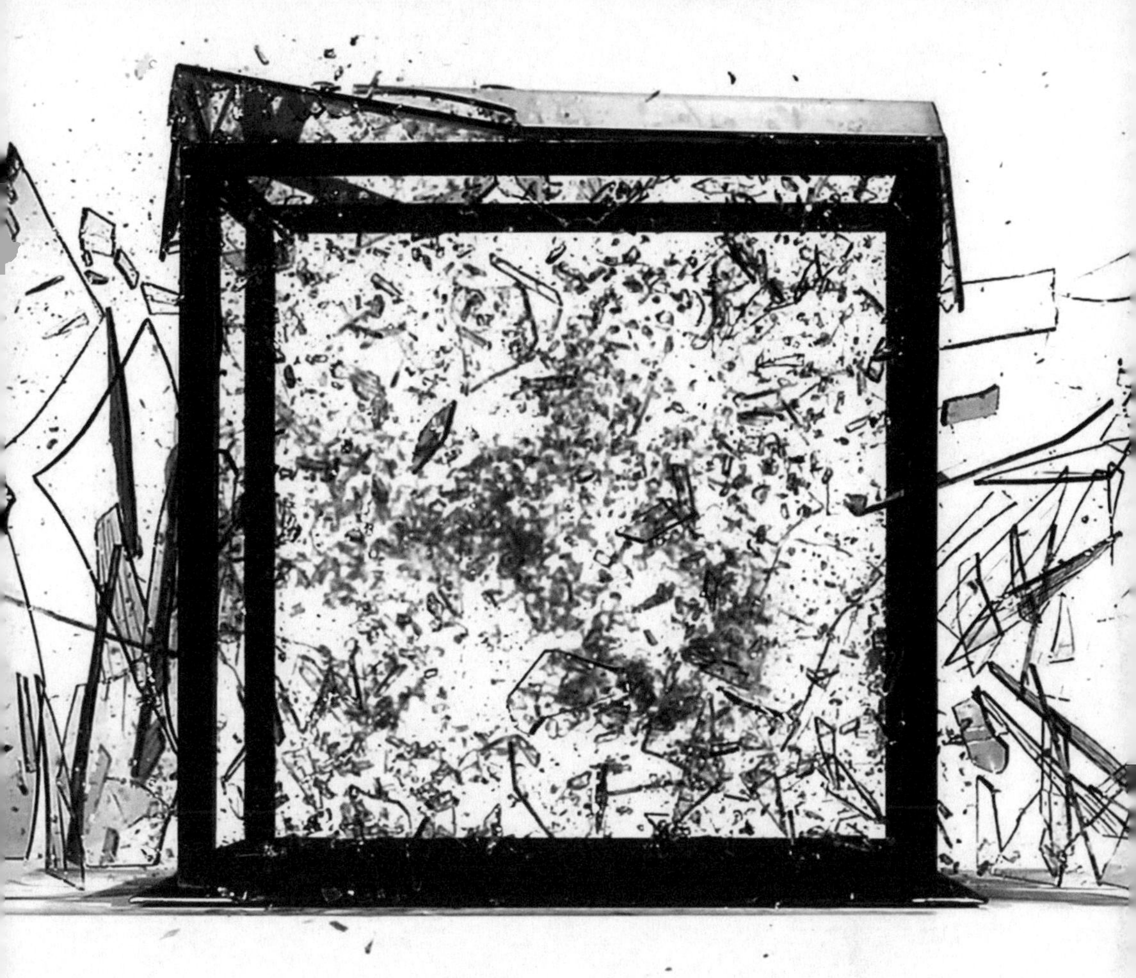

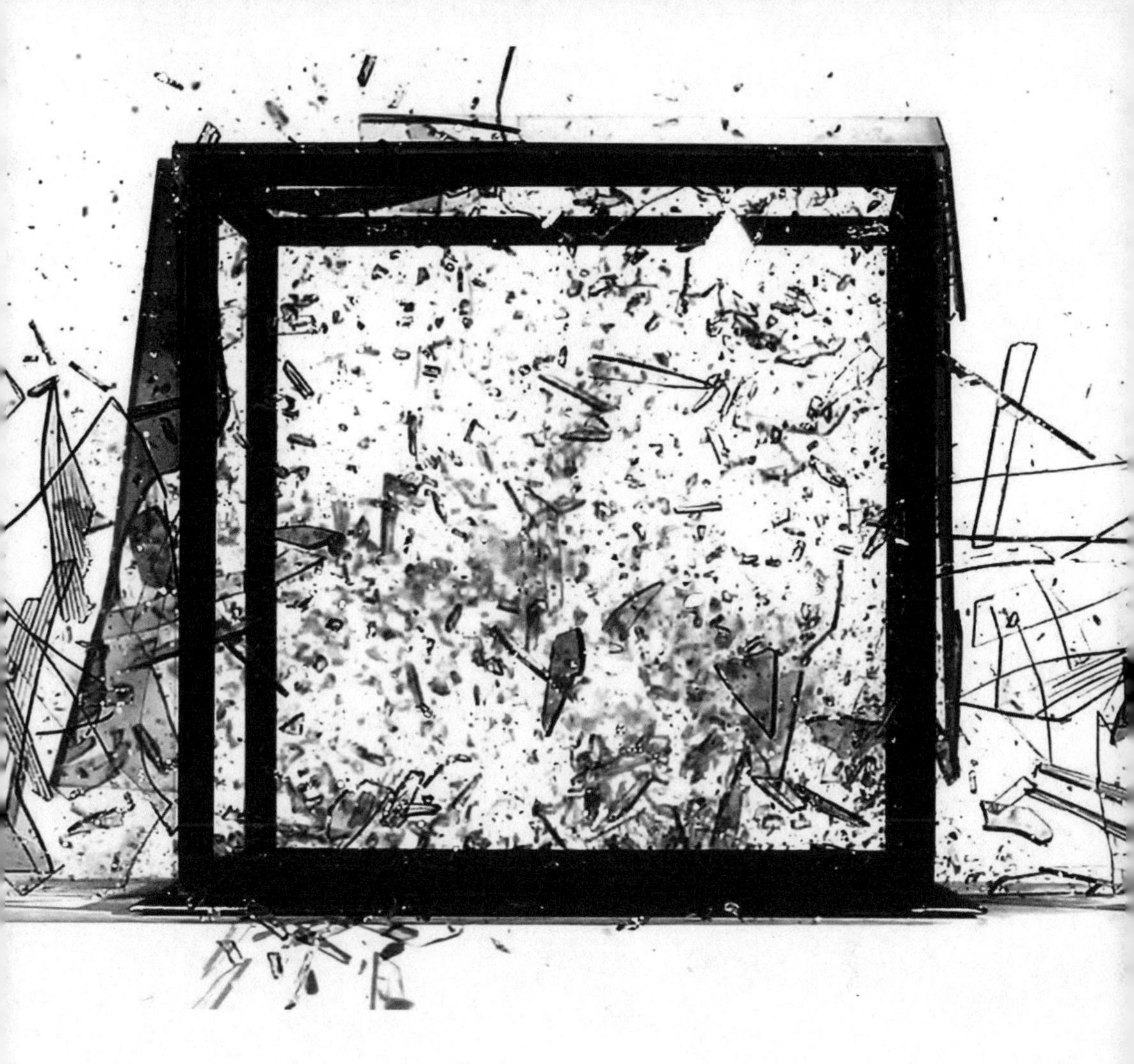

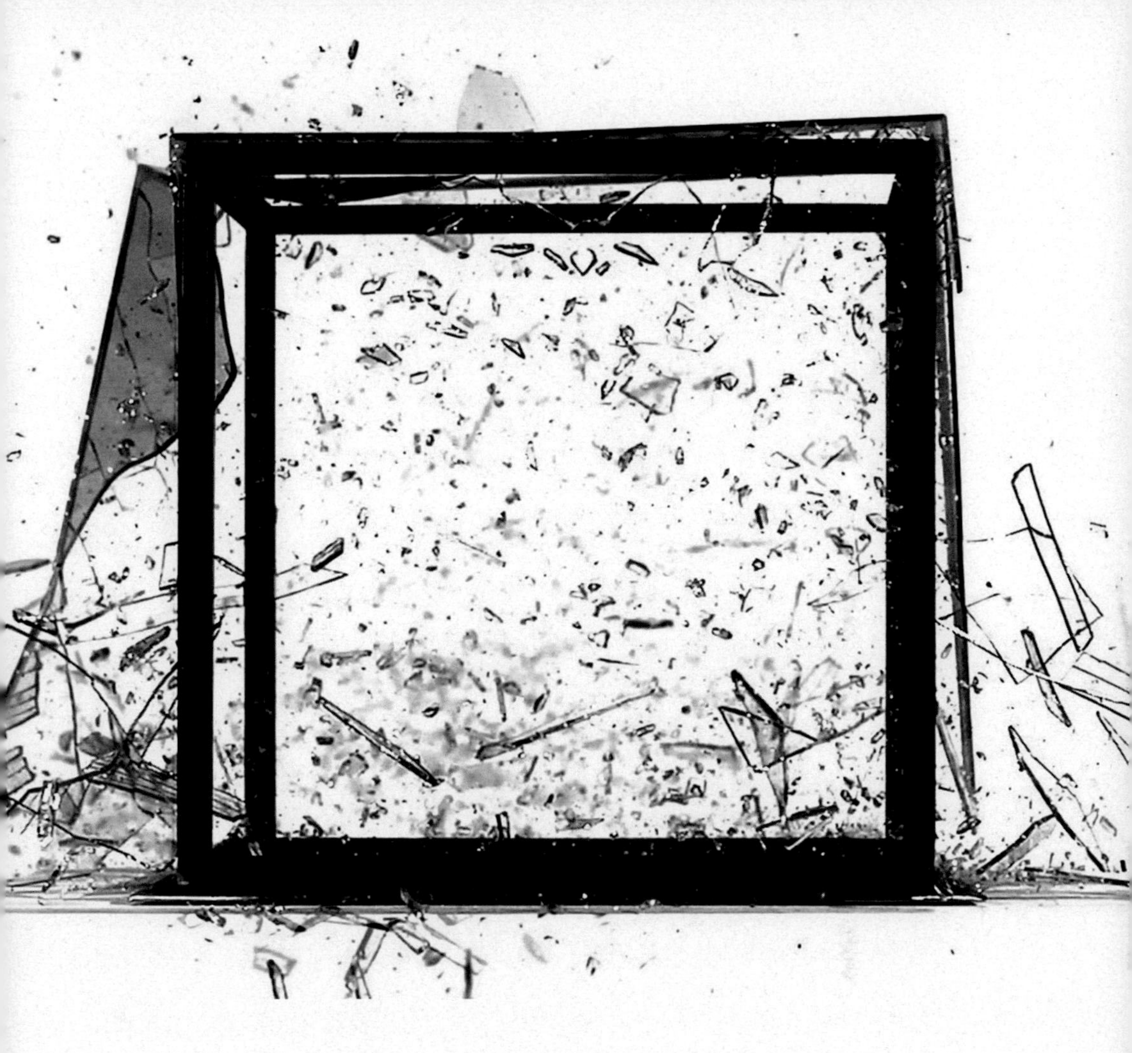

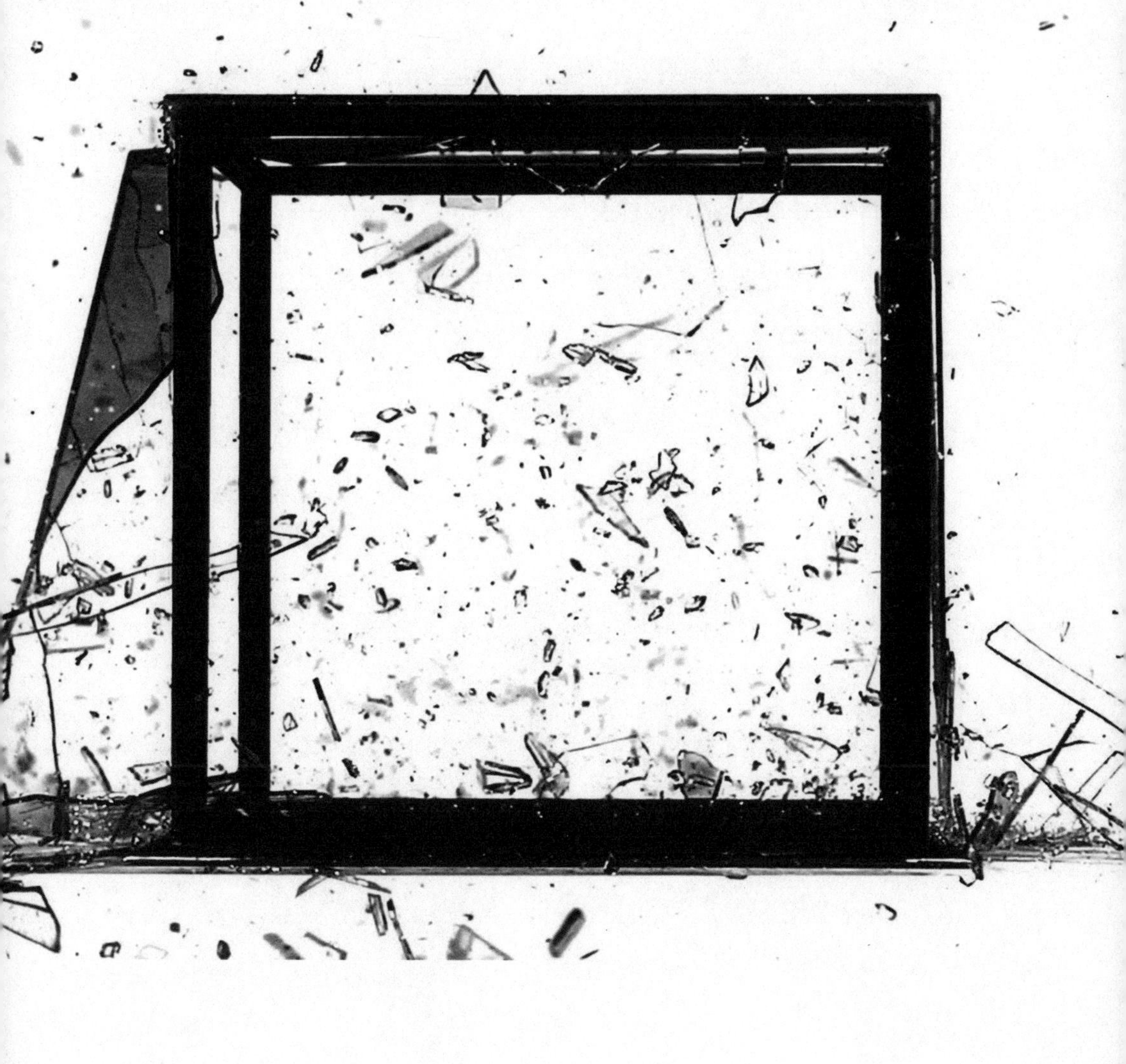

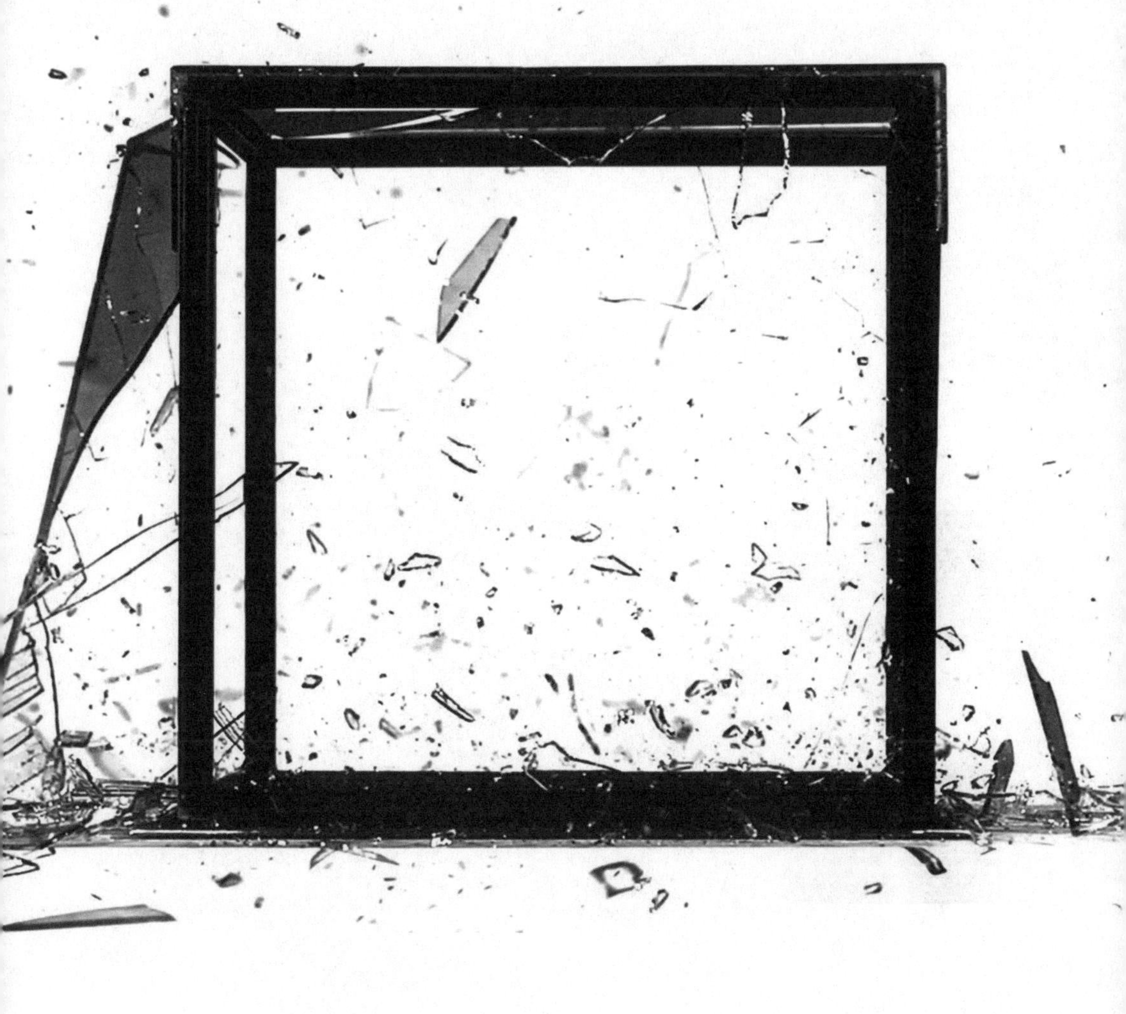

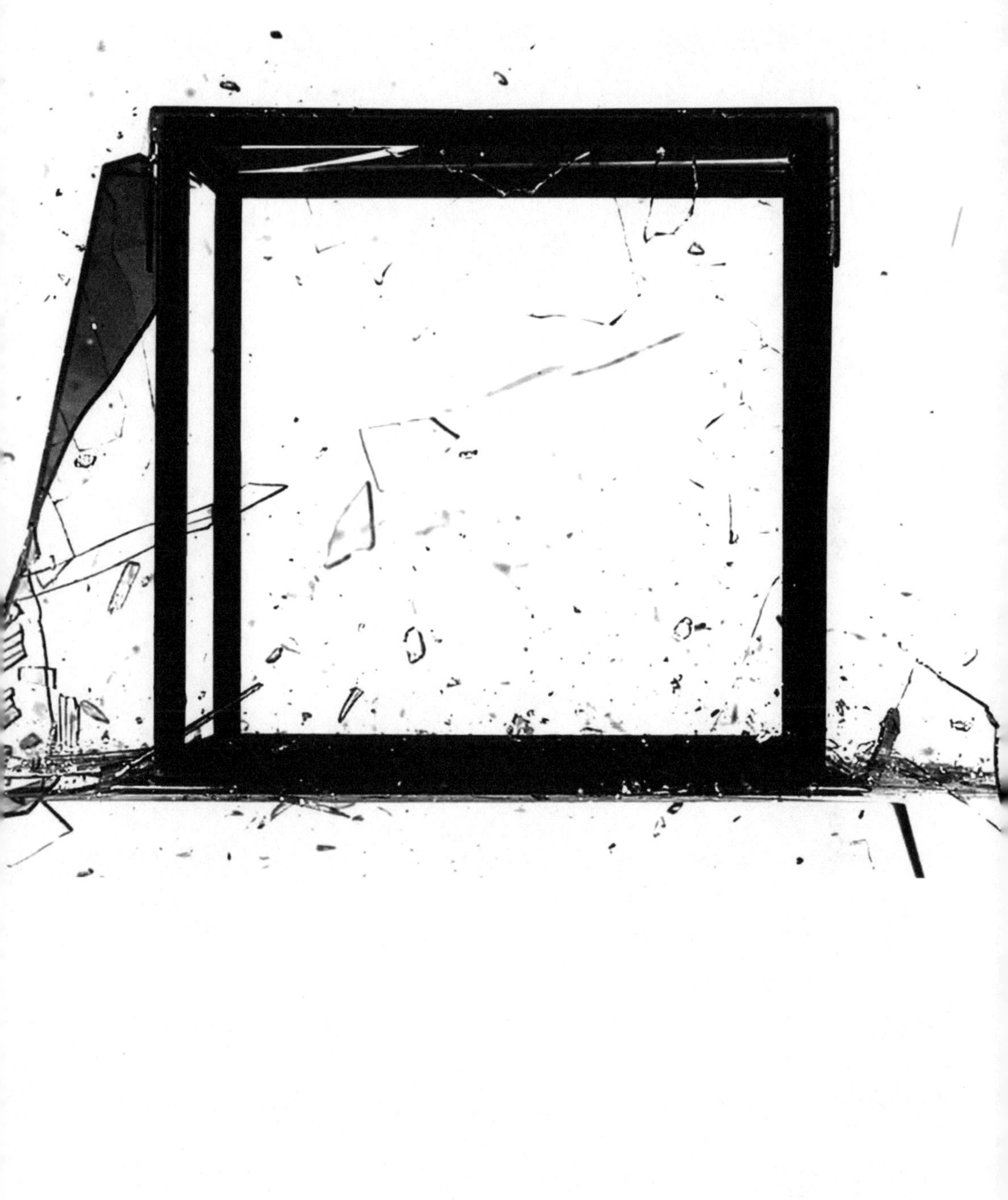

Video, color, sound,
6 mins

2005

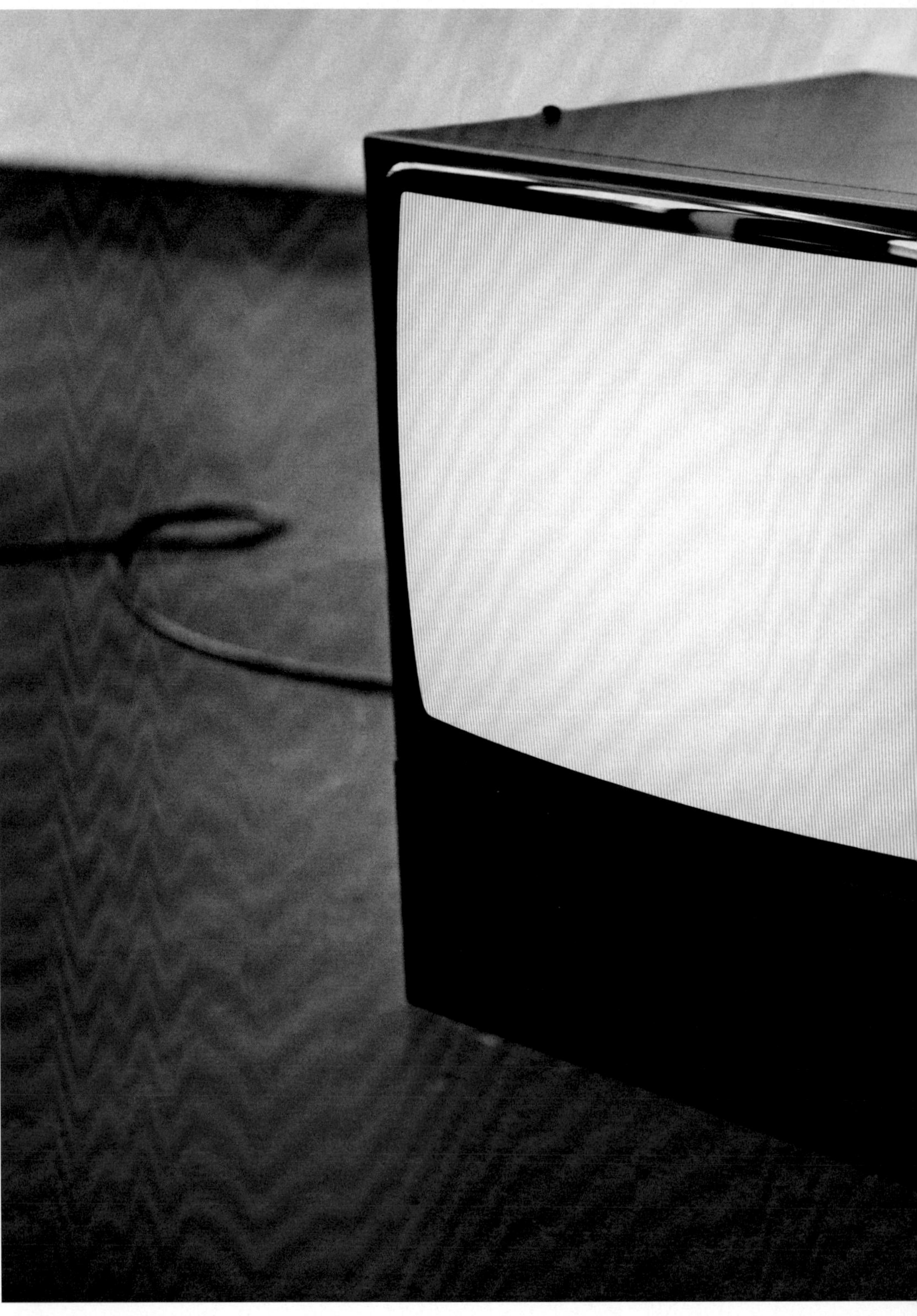

HANTAREX

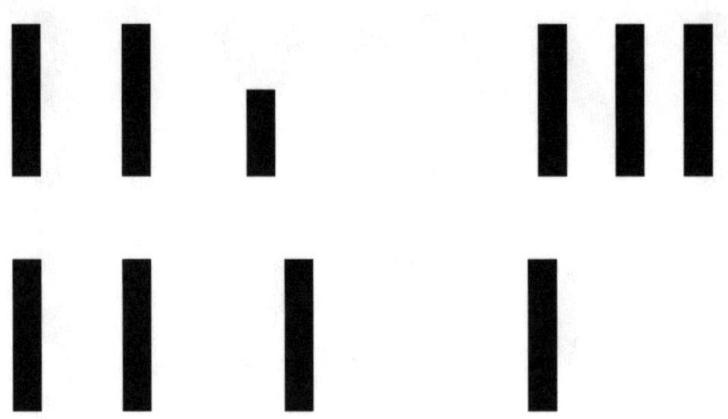

2010

Nano-sized grid on glass
168 x 84 cm

2010

Inkjet print on paper
42.5 x 35 cm, framed

LIVRO

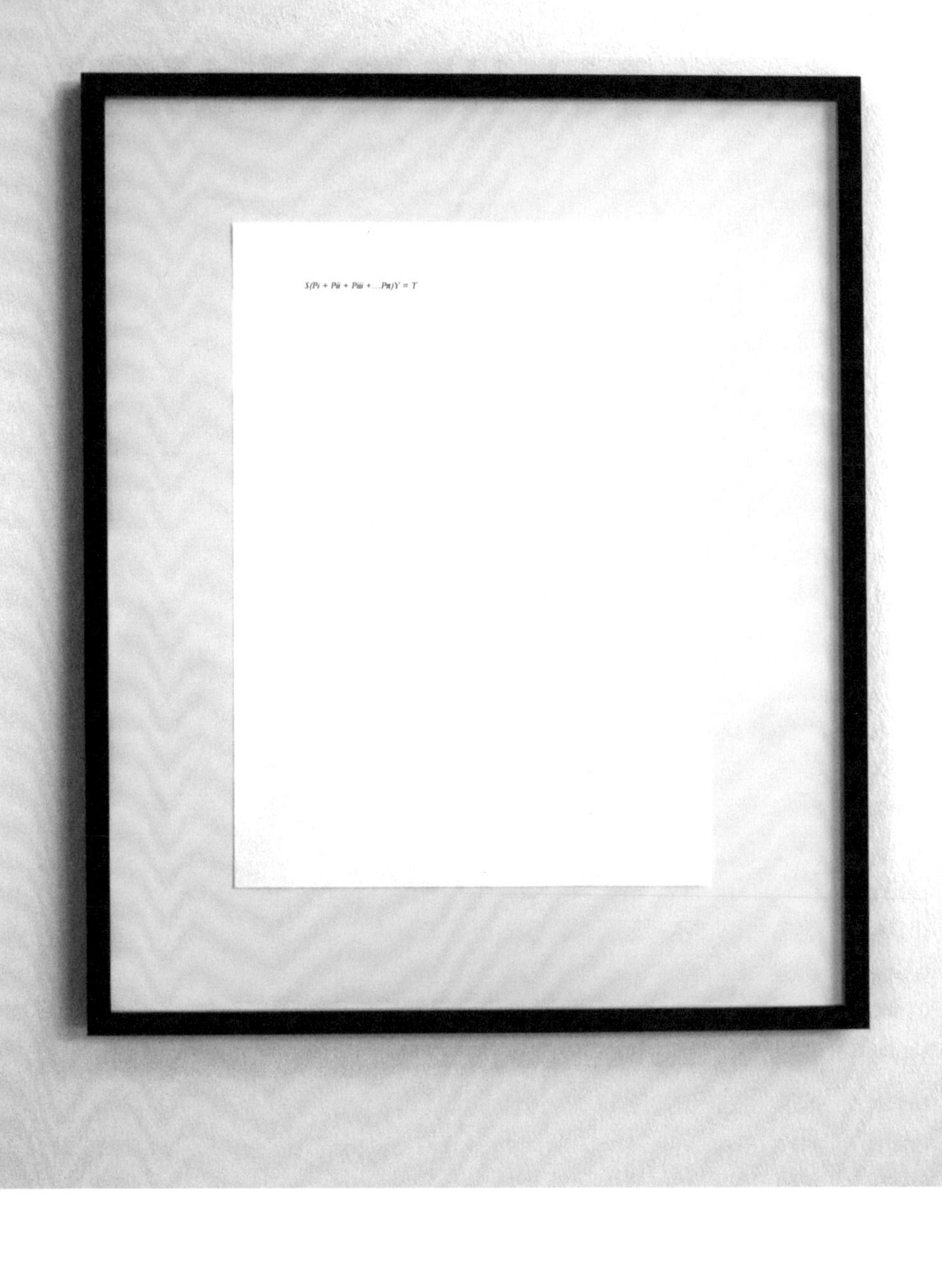

$S(P_i + P_{ii} + P_{iii} + \ldots P_n)Y = T$

VRO

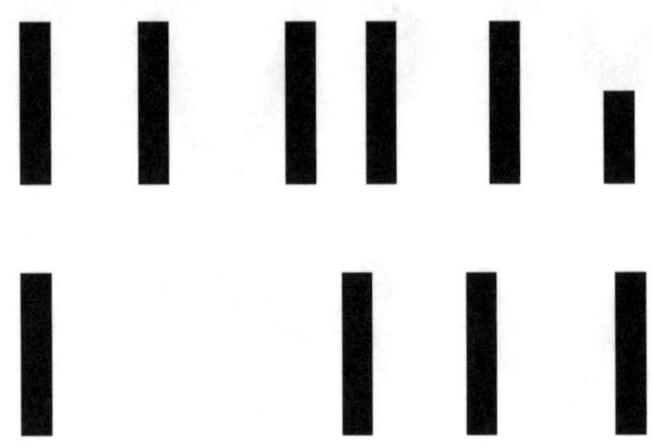

16mm film, black/white,
sound, 15 mins, projection
screen 66 x 90 cm

2008

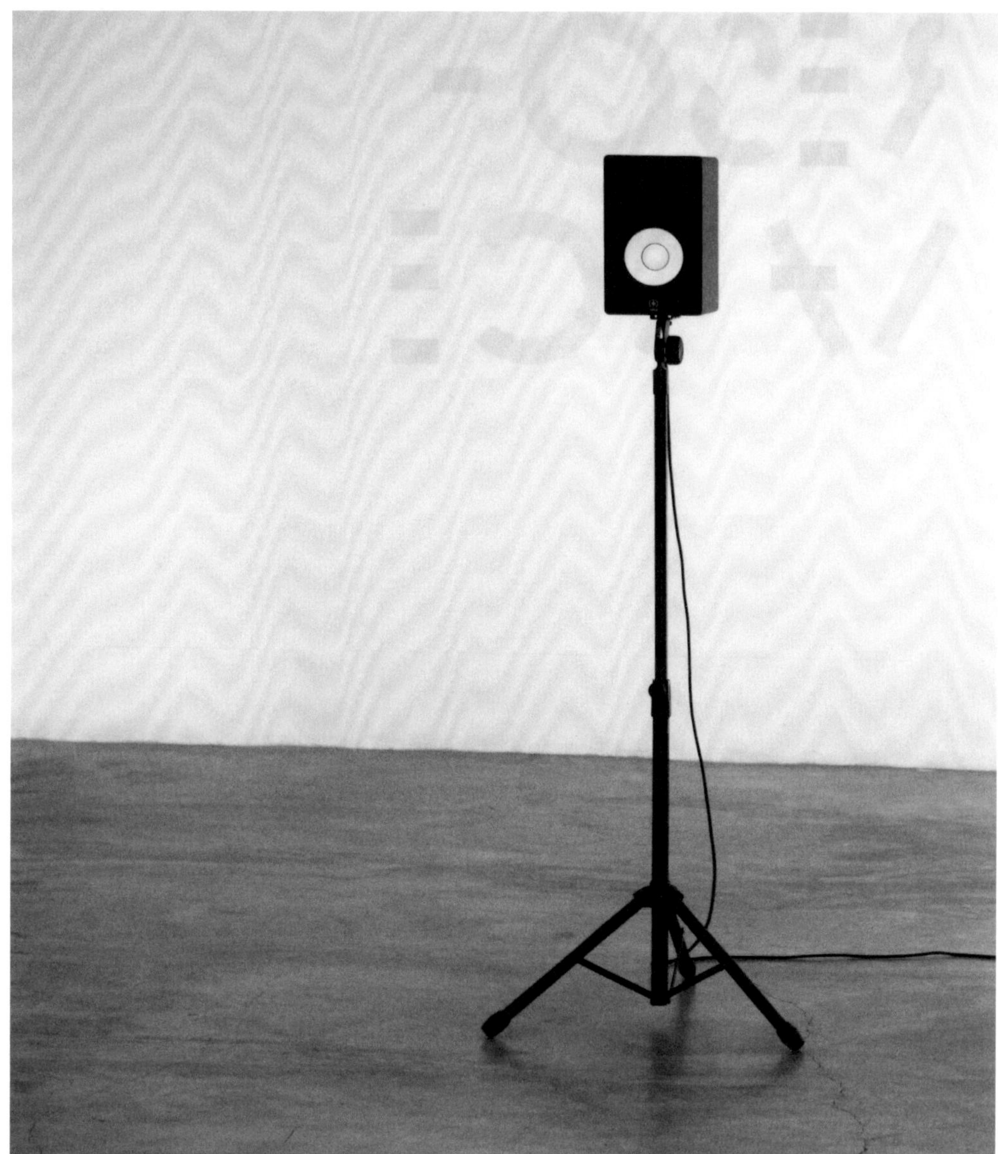

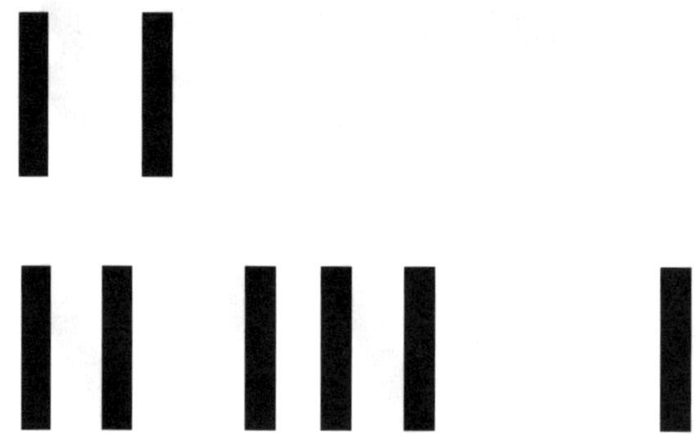

2006 – 2008

2 mobile phones,
pressure sensor, speakers
Dimensions variable

<u>between forms of representation and interpretation</u>
The permanent flickering of six lights transmits in coded form a statement of artistic intent; its sonic equivalent is heard simultaneously, running in and out of sync.

<u>modal patterns</u>
Two phrases: "more than the sum of its parts" and "a misshape of truth torments" are translated into audio-visual animations through a series of rendering processes, based on the Gestalt principles of perception. The first phrase, which appears recurrently in different contexts and in different guises, is, in this example, drawn from the pages of Roy Behrens' *Design in the Visual Arts* (1984, 49), which discusses Gestalt theory's influence on modern art and design. The second is an anagram of the first phrase.

<u>on the probability of an irregularity</u>
As part of a continuous and reconfigurable series under the same title, *on the probability of an irregularity* takes the form of a geometric metal structure that fires confetti from four holes at random intervals and in random sequences.

<u>0.</u>
A recorded image of a glass cube appears to be static and two-dimensional until it suddenly implodes to reveal the temporal and three-dimensional hidden nature of the predefined image.

<u>-./</u>
The index for the book, *Point and Line to Plane* (1926) by Wassily Kandinsky, is delivered as an audio-visual image via Morse code.

<u>beyond black</u>
A deliberately designed grid is perceivable only at nanometre scale; otherwise, the surface of the glass plate appears as a black, reflective, monochrome image.

<u>formula</u>
$S(Pi + Pii + Piii +...P\pi)Y = T$ is a mathematical formula for the creative process put forward by the Russian critic Nikolai Punin during a series of lectures in Petrograd in the summer of 1919 and entitled"Pervyi tsikl lektsii" ("First Cycle of Lectures").

<u>empty form</u>
A 16mm film projects only a black frame onto a small screen during a recitation of Kazimir Malevich's essay "Художник и кино" ("The Artist and The Cinema") as the soundtrack.

<u>resonance</u>
A repetitive beat is heard as its own exhibit. The sound is the artist's pulse relayed in real time, throughout the duration of the exhibition, irrespective of geographical location.

What happened to being at the end of modernity? What's the last person left with? Commercially producing, lost in a web of the multi? What is or might be our purpose in being (teleology) and what might be the being of being (ontology)? This, specifically explored as technocracy, goes beyond our intrinsic being: our intrinsic, ideologically framed and socially motivated early modern purpose to being became dictated by technology as a technocratic, extrinsic purpose to being. How can we live within this being?

<u>Where we are</u>
Modern reconstruction drove us into constructions of feasibility. A world we imagined to be tangible, through this very feasibility, summed up the will of the multitude: their various constructive specializations and contributory efforts. It is within this sphere that our purpose in being became dominant, our world narrowed to the single, anthropocentric perspective of souls.

The web spins the wheel. Physical particles circulate through abstract complexity. What once was analogue became digital, real connections became virtual ones. From metal to bits: what seemed to be tangible ended up being a work mode of the alienated production of being. The bigger picture, on the being of being, lost track of our framework. Things weren't so simple anymore; we were unable to leave the chain of being dictated by purpose.

Post-modernism introduced the confusion of being by accepting the deconstruction of our intrinsic purposes and responsibilities and by playing with and enjoying the extrinsic diversity of particles. Ideology failed, fundamental being fell into neglect and we hid in scenarios. A booming scene of technology nerds along with unstable, electronic/digital media and seemingly endless ranges of coded forms playing with the parameters of the scope of the absolute. These technological endeavours were often brash and barely managed to infect the intrinsic being of our lives, but they infected our extrinsic sensations of the technocratic unknown. This was very apparent in the 2011 GLOW light-art festival, which coincidentally included work by Andrés Ramírez Gaviria. As was evident here, people at ease with their take on purpose don't bother with intrinsic quests for materialisation, but they do crave extrinsic technological promises by technologically dictated matter when they are overwhelmed by them. Meanwhile, a scene of alternatives, including many artists, lined up to voice the inherent fruits of the intrinsic via craft, material tactility and the recent rise of the amateur's call to direct, sincere and low-end egalitarian anarchy.

The intrinsic is at play here: if our imagination's responsibilities are neglected we cannot exploit its productive mode. Our intrinsic sense of purpose is circulating around the lure of deconstruction and anarchy, conservatively turning to analogue being, while our extrinsic one is becoming digital and technocratic. Basically this adds together a production of being through emotional confusion and epistemological deviation.

<u>Between Forms of Representation and Interpretation</u>
We're surrounded by data, wrapped up in bodies of interpretation. As utterance, forms are primarily speech acts. They manifest themselves (locutionary acts). As such, right there at that moment, objects formed by humans – artefacts – first of all relate. Like any other artefact, the physical nature of Andrés Ramírez

Gaviria's work releases a voice through production: it suggests meaning and activates interpretation. The signs of this body can be read beyond the implicit and the sense of what so far has been unconscious, turning it into an embodiment that is conscious and aware (illocutionary act).

Although we might be lost in translation, puzzled and unable to read the algorithms or reach out to the presumed absolute of the motives that produced the artefacts in the first place, we enhance our sense of belonging within this very body, without reaching the level of dominance.

I've always been greeted with a feeling of frustration when I'm faced with Gaviria's work. He doesn't allow the logic of the algorithm, the programmed texts, variously coded in his works (hidden behind intensely flashing light bars in between forms of representation and interpretation) to speak out, to reveal their message. I'm more practically inclined and feel I need to be left with a tangible result (perlocutionary act). Nevertheless, the complexity of the locutionary act in these works is too complex to read – except perhaps for the technocratic autistic. Only the implied idea of meaning, an intention of communication manifested artistically, a voice that acts via the senses of the body of technology comes through. But that is actually the artist's intention: you're not relating to any message, you're relating to the motives that leave you between forms of representation and interpretation.

Where to go, in here?
It takes courage to tackle the challenges thrown up by this state of disorder. It requires the ability to speak in between languages of the intrinsic and the extrinsic beyond the analogue and the digital, ignoring both coded and un-coded communication but voicing the relation that is the sum of this being; to release the particles not through themselves, but to position them in themselves. To hold a mirror up to this scene that is neutral to both intrinsic and extrinsic purposes, accessible for both to grasp, requires being sound in this sum. Highly political, beyond the order of what

we are and how we've made our being, into a void of the unknown, Andrés Ramírez Gaviria's work allows for ontological dynamics, relying upon technological poetics and people's ability to situate themselves within this being's settings through responsive sensory capacities. When aware and adoptive, both intrinsic and extrinsic acts can expand our being through them. This would run through our being instead of through operating: altering the purpose of acts into processes of sensibility. Did we just commute our extrinsic... Is the connection made?

Damn...I really have to buy that Ipad to access and see for myself: I don't want to be such a dreadfully conservative, art-minded sicko...

"The thing about perfection is that it's unknowable. It's impossible, but it's also right in front of us all the time. You wouldn't know that because I didn't when I created you."

These words are from the final encounter between CLU and his creator in the second part of the science-fiction film *Tron* (2010), directed by Joseph Kosinsky and produced by Steven Lisberger, who directed the first film in 1982. The dialogue refers to the fact that CLU, with the incomplete concepts that he had inherited from his father-creator-programmer but had no tools for updating, became a predatory tyrant, even though, like his creator, he lived by the ideal of generating systems for a perfect world.

Despite the fact that references such as minimalism and modern abstract creation are decisive in Andrés Ramírez Gaviria's work, it is crucial to understand the many allusions the artist makes to these works - and to the critical systems that followed them in some way - as part of another world view that already bears little resemblance to the conceptual frameworks and circumstances that inspired and sustained both those approaches and the reactions they produced and confronted.

Any interest in geometry in distinguished contemporary artistic practice, starting from a consideration of history, demands that meaning be unravelled from the tools it resorts to and the context to which it belongs. Geometry and mathematics are always anchored in perfection but that does not mean that they are closed concepts or confined to the limits of objectivity. In this sense it is clear that the use of these tools is not devoid of emotional situations that are generally ignored in the case of abstract geometry.

The work of Andrés Ramírez Gaviria, like that of many artists from his generation, is wholly committed to recent advances in science, technology and cybernetics. This sole motive in many cases goes beyond the meanings, searches and theorisations that have been set up around modernity and its contradictions.

The technological progress and inquiry on which the artist bases his work are the outcome of views of reality that have broken through the boundaries encircling thought and aesthetics of the third, and later the fourth, dimension heralded by Einstein and acknowledged at the most basic level in relation to the concept of relativity. This surely implies that the images used in Andrés Ramírez Gaviria's work are interwoven with inquiries that are more all-encompassing, complex and distant from the idea of relativity and also of the simultaneity that stimulated so many 20th century changes in attitude and thinking.

An single-focused view of the current communications scenario and the repositionings produced in this area in the way knowledge and information are handled can provide powerful images about the shift in meaning of notions such as time, simultaneity and relativity. This is even more true if a comparison is set up with the connection advantages offered up to a few years ago by lower capacity systems. Relationships, landscapes, political and natural boundaries, needs, references and the very place inhabited constantly undergo drastic change with each new imaginarium used.

It is not about stating that there is currently a clear assimilation of those events and of the bases on which they rest, or that something similar had happened before. The most significant discoveries, the ones that lead humanity towards other perspectives and possibilities, trigger at the same time a multitude of chaotic events and, to that extent, they take place between contradictory exchanges.

Any discovery, on whatever scale, takes place between slow and rapid steps forward, as if between acceptance and resistance, resulting in scarce or exceptional opportunities for clearly recording the processes of change at conscious or programmed level. This means that the most intelligent analyses of the cause and determining factors of intellectual and cultural products are those that break through the host of reasons that interweave themselves in unexpected and paradoxical ways among the most imperceptible understandings, passions and intuitions.

It is vital to deduce from many angles how the shifts in meaning come about, in which connections, and in the midst of what kind of correct or incorrect interpretations.

Today, the creed of art as political commitment is finally showing its age. The concept reached its pinnacle in the decades between the 1930s and the 1990s, resulting, more often than not, in fanatical and facile distortions. It has been replaced by blind faith in the saving communion between art and science, which has already taken hold in a variety of ways at other times in history, with many examples of reductionisms that have culminated in confusing and sometimes tyrannical forms.

One of the most recent examples of this trend occurred in the period between the mid-19th and mid-20th century. The start of this historical period hinted at another reality of time led by research and the processes set in motion by industrialisation and by the appearance of photography among other products of knowledge.

The impressionists were the first to clarify, long before science, that a view was beginning to develop in which reality was perceived as relative and therefore unstable, abstract and indefinable, bringing them back to the place where the most emphatic message was being expressed in the sphere of poetry. They were modern pioneers in understanding that neither science nor perfection of techniques could reveal complete truths in their individual fields. At the same time, they understood that the scientific advances they were feeding on were in turn being fed by the revelations that studious lovers of harmony and truth were able to make.

Five decades later, the logical consequence of impressionist relativism was abstract geometry, the search for measurement and for the rule of ultimate balance that can make the ephemeral and the unstable remain through setting up recreative cycles. In the meantime, contradictory groups, their judgement clouded by objective knowledge, declared the end of painting and even of art itself. Other views chose to announce that art was reborn and veered more towards the empirical sciences, finally flowing out into various expressions of Fascism.

The revelations made by the vague and constantly fading images conjured up by 19th century visionaries took shape as mathematical formulae in the two first decades of the 20th century. The repositioning that this entailed was so huge that it took more than two decades to be absorbed in the spheres of greater educational refinement and adapted to everyday life.

But despite the radically changing approaches to the physical world and even though scientific, social and even natural reflections were loudly expressing it, the theoretical bases of fields of knowledge did not vary accordingly, not even in the most critical dynamics. These dynamics continued to drag old ways of understanding the world that had been left behind, which resulted in a gradual broadening of a discursive chaos that would keep many social, scientific, cultural and aesthetic forms and processes bogged down in a painful kind of mannerism.

Understanding the way reality worked in the fourth dimension was in many ways a massive challenge, even for privileged minds, so the ideal of the relativity of time and space was embedded in discourse that contradicted it. The task of rebuilding the world according to new dimensions is so vast that, although more than a century has elapsed since the fourth was proved, the majority of the mechanics of human creation continue to operate in third dimensional logic.

Of course, artistic production and discourse have not escaped the confusion. Radical early 20th century works, such as those by Marcel Duchamp, Pablo Picasso and Vassily Kandinsky, have not been completely understood and therefore not bettered. They clearly exercised untold influence, but certainly not because of their deepest and truest message. The chemistry between these artists and the leading observers of their day and those from whom they inherited pioneering interpretations and forms had such a huge impact that it catapulted them outside their fellows and placed their perspective within reach of very few. They understood the physical world and everything built on it in a higher dimension than had hitherto been accepted. That dimension on which the pillars of the 20th century came into being was the fourth and with it, many operations in geometry and mathematics were redefined. Whether it is understood or not, the outlook on everything changed with the force of attraction they exercised on other practices and processes.

At present, the new pioneers claim that another seven dimensions exist. That makes eleven or twelve, or even more. The leap taken by many forms that have sensed and embraced them for several decades in various fields and advances is therefore immeasurably more powerful than the one that took place in the 20th century, which as yet has not been fully absorbed. So it is sheer fantasy to speculate on the requirement to be up to date with the future and, therefore, also indispensable to observe and attend to the potential insertion of new options that will develop more naturally by those who perceive them most closely.

Works such as those by Andrés Ramírez Gaviria navigate these new waters in a formation as yet unnamed because there is still too little awareness about what developments it is making or what its features will be. Artists like him are on the brink of a new perspective leading to an unpredictable reappraisal of reality. But they are out there with the advantage of their conviction that there can be no balanced truth without subjectivity. This can be understood clearly in Andrés Ramírez Gaviria's work. It sends out powerful images about the constrictions of objective approaches and of the serious shortcomings of studies in which there is no healthy circulation between the outer and the inner world, or even in which this procedure is regarded as unnecessary. This artist's work is always an exact fusion between technological improvement and broadening of knowledge, with errors and limitations in the translation, frontiers of the objective gaze and mysteries of the space within; of what is never understood or known by means of geometric and mathematical operations and therefore always taking us by surprise when it breaks out.

In this sense, this artist's work is a constant and wise revealer of secrets, in the habit of keeping to itself any information that inspires continuity. The greatest of these secrets, the definition of perfection, the driving force behind Andrés Ramírez Gaviria's work, can be understood in its search as the changing and inextricably multiple and complex structure that underlies all events and that wants to be known, but always turns out to be slippery and impossible to encode.

ONOMATOPEE 49

Research Project
between forms of representation and interpretation

Editors
Freek Lomme and
Andrés Ramírez Gaviria

**Project management
and exhibition curator**
Freek Lomme

Texts
Freek Lomme
María A. Lovino

Graphic design
Lesley Moore

Printing
Lecturis

**Translations and
proofreading**
QualityCom 2007,
S.L.U

PHOTOGRAPHY
Exhibition
**Onomatopee / between
forms of representation
and interpretation**
Peter cox

beyond black
Emilio Quintero

**on the probability of an
irregularity**
Emilio Quintero

empty form
Gerardo Suárez

-./
Jürgen Kranzler

resonance
Fer Figheras

PROJECT CREDITS
empty form
Voice by Lev Manovich

0.
Realized with the
support of Matthias
Uiberacker

modal patterns
Realized with the
support of Jörg Piringer

Paper
Da costa
Core Gloss

Edition
500

Made possible thanks to
Municipality of Eindhoven,
Mondriaan Fund and BMUKK

Special thanks to
Mareike Bremer
Jürgen Kranzler

Onomatopee
Bleekstraat 23
NL 5611 VB Eindhoven
The Netherlands
www.onomatopee.net
info@onomatopee.net

© 2012, Onomatopee

ISBN: 978-90-78454-85-4

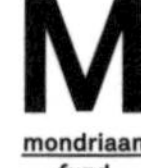
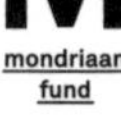

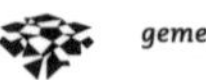